Artful Polymer Clay

Techniques for stylish jewelry and décor

Gail Ritchey

D1368246

KALMBACH BOOKS

Kalmbach Books
21027 Crossroads Circle
Waukesha, Wisconsin 53186
www.Kalmbach.com/Books

© 2009 by Gail Ritchey

Published in 2009

13 12 11 10 09   1 2 3 4 5

Manufactured in the United States of America

ISBN: 978-0-87116-282-3

Publisher's Cataloging-in-Publication Data
Ritchey, Gail, 1950-
  Artful polymer clay : techniques for stylish jewelry and decor / by Gail Ritchey.

  p. : col. ill. ; cm.

  ISBN: 978-0-87116-282-3

1. Polymer clay craft--Handbooks, manuals, etc. 2. Jewelry making--Handbooks, manuals, etc. 3. Decoration and ornament. I. Title.

TT297 .R58 2009
745.594

CONTENTS

12

32

59

74

INTRODUCTION

It's so exhilarating to play, shape, and mold with polymer clay! Clay is easy to use, and the results are breathtaking. With this book, I want to introduce you to polymer clay and show you some of the gorgeous pieces you can make. If you're a beginner, no worries—you'll be molding and shaping in no time.

If you've got some experience already, you can use polymer clay to create just about anything. Shape projects made entirely of clay, or cover an old glass vase with clay to update the look of your living room. Design jewelry, home décor items, accessories, or anything else you can imagine. You can even use clay to create bookmarks and drawer pulls.

Polymer clay is affordable, and that's the beauty of this medium: You can make almost anything you can imagine, and it won't cost an arm and a leg. You can try all of the techniques in this book without worrying about the cost of your experiments. After you finish shaping your polymer piece, you can just bake it in a toaster oven.

When you are comfortable with the basics, you can advance to more complex techniques, like mokume gane. Polymer clay can be used to create many different looks, and the projects in this book are just examples. Please try other colors and experiment with all of the different types of clay. Ignite your own creativity with the great projects in this book, and then branch out on your own to explore this versatile medium, if you like.

I have been working with clay for years, and I haven't run out of ideas yet. I want to share some of what I have learned along the way, so I included tips explaining how to fix some of the problems that can occur. You'll find detailed instructions for completing each piece beautifully as well as inspiration in my showcase designs included at the end of each chapter.

There are very few hard-and-fast rules in working with polymer clay. Play around, have fun, and try all kinds of new techniques. You might be surprised at the beautiful items you make!

BASICS

About Polymer Clay

Polymer clay is a synthetic medium that cures by baking in a home oven. It comes in many colors, all of which can be mixed to create an almost unlimited array of shades. Polymer clay is wonderfully resilient, pliable, and easy to mold into any shape. When baked, it becomes strong and firm but not brittle.

There are many different brands of polymer clays. Some of the clays are Kato Polyclay, FIMO Classic and FIMO Soft, Cernit, Premo, Studio Clay, and Pardo. Any of these clays can be used for the projects in this book. Polymer clay doesn't shrink much; the biggest change in polymer clay from its uncured to cured state is the extreme color change some of the brands undergo. Test-bake a piece of clay, if desired, to make sure you like the final color.

Polymer clay blends with inks, dyes, and pigments. Kato Polyclay also has color concentrates. Add a small amount of concentrate to regular polymer clay to change and mix colors. Polymer clay can be painted and used to cover glass, metal, and papier-mâché objects. However, you will get inconsistent results trying to cover wood. Because of the moisture level in wood, it expands and shrinks when heated. During heating, the wood creates air bubbles that rise into the clay surrounding it, and the clay may crack. (I have tried coating the wood with paint and glue with mixed results. The best solution is to cover the wood with metal tape to block out air bubbles, but that doesn't always work. Just keep this in mind if you want to use wood.)

In addition to standard clay, you can experiment with liquid polymer clay, a fluid medium. Use liquid clay to add a different look to a clay piece (see p. 39 for a pendant-and-earrings set made with liquid clay). Colored liquid clays are also available.

tip

I prefer Kato Polyclay because of its strength, its consistency (both in color and texture) from block to block, and its packaging with a vacuum seal. Most importantly, its color doesn't change from the raw clay to the baked product.

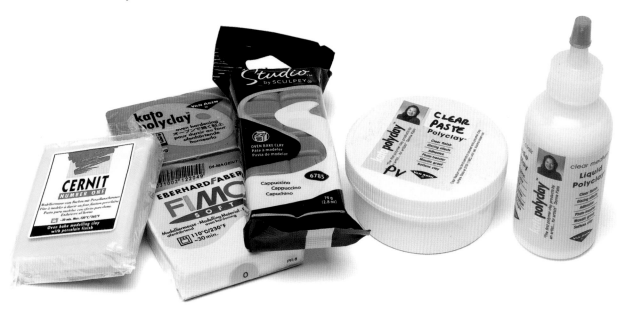

Conditioning Polymer Clay

Before you begin to work with polymer clay, the clay must be conditioned. When polymer clay sits, the ingredients separate and need to be mixed again. Conditioning strengthens and warms up the clay, making it easier to work with and shape.

Work on a large, smooth, flat surface. Do not use a wooden table, as clay will stick to the grain of the wood and ruin the finish; use a plastic or ceramic surface instead. Keep your hands and all surfaces clean. Polymer clay seems to attract dirt, and the light colors will show soiling.

Unless listed otherwise, you'll want to condition one block of each clay color to make the projects in this book. Some of the pieces will use only a small amount of a clay block. Use your judgment to determine the amount of clay you need before you begin.

Conditioning by Hand

Polymer clay can be conditioned by hand without a clay machine. To hand-condition polymer clay, flatten it with an acrylic roller. Fold and roll it with the roller again, and repeat 20–25 times until the clay is warm and supple. You can also knead the clay with your hands in any way that is comfortable for you. Try creating logs, twisting the clay, or forming it into a pancake or ball and squashing it flat.

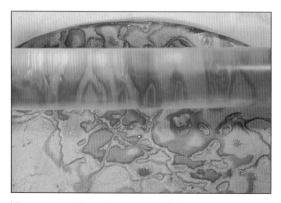

Use an acrylic roller to condition by hand.

tip

Trapped air pockets will ruin a project. Take care when conditioning clay to pick out any air pockets that develop with a needle tool (see p. 8). When forming a shape, try to remove the air. If you discover air bubbles after baking, press them out while the clay is still warm. If necessary, prick the bubbles to remove the air, and then press the clay smooth. Also, baking an item upside-down helps eliminate bubbles.

Using a Clay Machine

If you plan on doing a lot of work with polymer clay, a clay machine will pay for itself quickly in the time and trouble saved. There are many brands of clay and pasta machines available.

tip

If the clay is too dry, add a drop or two of liquid clay to moisten it. If the clay is very soft, floppy, and hard to handle, place the sheet of clay between sheets of plain paper and allow the paper to absorb the excess moisture.

1. Cut the clay block into slices just slightly thicker than the thickest setting of the clay machine.

When using a clay machine, start on the thickest setting and step down one setting at a time to get to a thinner setting. The medium (3/64 in./1.2 mm) setting is a good setting for conditioning clay. If you need a thicker sheet after conditioning, fold the sheet in half and set the clay machine at a lower setting, going one setting thicker each time.

Frequently wipe the rollers of your clay machine with a paper towel, especially the underside of the clay machine where the scrapers are, to remove any sticking clay. Clay machines all tend to have a slight difference in the space between the rollers, causing one side of the clay sheet to eventually become longer than the other side. When you fold the clay in half using your right hand, placing the clay in your left hand, use your left hand to place the fold on the rollers, and turn the clay. The clay that was on the right when folding gets placed on the left on the clay machine.

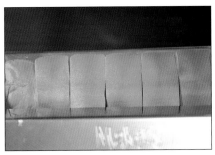

2. Place the slices against the rollers of a clay machine dedicated to clay, and turn the handle. Repeat if more clay is desired, and then run through the machine to combine all the slices into one sheet.

3. Fold the sheet in half.

4. Place the sheet fold-first against the rollers or on the side. (Never place a fold last, as air bubbles will get trapped in the clay.) Repeat steps 3 and 4 until the sheet is soft and thoroughly conditioned.

Clay Thickness Settings

These clay thickness settings are for a Makin's Ultimate Clay Machine and an Atlas. The #1 setting on both the Makin's and Atlas is the thickest setting; the setting gets thinner as the numbers get higher. Some of the other machine are reversed, with the #1 setting being the thinnest. Adjust the instructions to match your clay machine as needed.

#1	3/32 in. (.24 mm)	#6	1/32 in. (.8 mm)
#2	3/32 in. (.24 mm)	#7	1/64 in. (.4 mm)
#3	5/64 in. (.2 mm)	#8	< 1/64 in. (.4 mm)
#4	1/16 in. (1.6 mm)	#9	< 1/64 in. (.4 mm)
#5	3/64 in. (1.2 mm)		

Basic Clay Tools

Use several different kinds of rollers for conditioning and shaping clay. Silicone and rubber rollers will help smooth the clay, while acrylic and metal rollers are perfect for flattening the clay and making thin pieces. Dedicate all polymer clay tools for clay only; do not use them for food or other purposes.

tip

If desired, add a clay handle to make your needle tool easier to use. Wrap a sheet of clay around the tool handle, smooth, and bake.

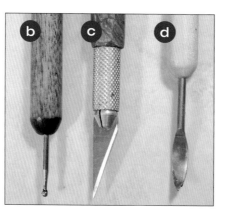
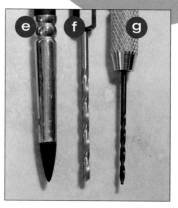

Use **needle tools** and **piercing pins (a)** to create fine, delicate holes. Use a **ball stylus (b)** to make holes or indentions in clay that are slightly larger than those created with a needle tool. Cut clay as needed with a sharp **craft knife (c)**. Wipe the blade with a wet wipe to remove any clay buildup as you work, or the clay buildup will tend to pull the clay being sliced. A **curved metal clay tool (d)** works well to smooth seams in clay. A **clay shaper (e)** is a rubber-tipped tool that comes in various shapes. Use it to smooth clay and get into areas that are difficult to reach with your fingers. You can drill clay beads by hand to enlarge holes in beads after baking. Use **drill bits (f, g)** in appropriate sizes to make the holes. Lastly, a **slicing blade (h)** is one of the most useful tools for cutting polymer clay. Cut strips from clay blocks and make straight cuts where needed. A slicing blade also gives a nice, smooth cut on the edges of items. This tool has a *very* sharp blade. Be careful to avoid cutting yourself with the sharp edge.

Molds and Texture Sheets

Polymer clay molds easily and shows great detail. Some of the different types of molds are shown here. Choose from rubber or plastic (you can also use cookie molds). You may need a release agent, such as water or powder, to help remove the clay from the forms, especially for the plastic molds. Spray the mold with a fine mist of water or brush the mold with a fine dusting of baby powder or cornstarch. Some molds, such as Kraft Lady molds, have a built-in release agent.

Texture sheets also work great with polymer clay. The sheets shown are a plastic texture sheet (this will require a release agent—see above), and various rubber texture sheets or stamps. Other items that can be used to texture polymer clay are kitchen scrubbies, towels, coarse sandpaper, and fabric.

Polymer clay tends to attract dust and pet hair, so keep unbaked items covered with plastic wrap. Store unused clay in plastic bags by color families or in a scrap clay bag. Clay lasts for up to a year, so don't throw away your scraps!

Baking Polymer Clay

To cure polymer clay, bake it in an oven or toaster oven for the manufacturer's recommended time. Most clay labels recommend baking for a certain number of minutes for a specific clay thickness. I usually bake clay pieces for one hour. If baking times are not given in the instructions, bake at the recommended temperature for one hour. Baking time is flexible, but the longer clay is baked, the stronger it is. Baked polymer clay also hardens as it cools. Baking temperature varies by brand. If your items break, you probably need to increase the baking time.

Bake the clay you are using at the temperature recommended on the package. Since oven temperatures can vary greatly, it is best to check your oven temperature with a thermometer.

Many people prefer to use a clay-dedicated counter-top oven instead of the oven they use for food. If you bake the clay in your home oven, use a light or timer to remind you that the clay is baking. Polymer clay will burn if baked at a higher temperature than

recommended, and it could release toxic fumes. If this happens, turn the oven off, open some windows, and let the house air out.

Place items to be baked on a ceramic tile covered with polyester batting. A ceramic tile is a great, inexpensive work surface, and it can be put in the oven to bake your clay without having to move the clay. This is my surface of choice. Polymer clay will become shiny where it touches a flat surface during baking, and using polyester batting under the clay will keep this from happening (it's especially noticeable with white or translucent clay). If you are concerned about fumes, dedicate a covered roaster to your clay use, or cover the clay with a tightly crimped tent of aluminum foil.

You can add unbaked clay to baked clay to embellish a piece. If the unbaked clay doesn't want to stick to the baked clay, brush a tiny amount of liquid clay or Polyglue on it, let the liquid sit for a minute, and then add the unbaked clay. Rebake as needed.

Finishing

Enlarging a hole in a clay bead

A polymer clay bead can be easily drilled to enlarge the hole. Choose a drill bit slightly larger than the hole, and twist the drill by hand. Repeat with a larger drill bit, if necessary.

Sanding

You can sand and buff baked polymer clay to a high shine. Start with a fine-grit (220) sandpaper, unless the clay is rough (if so, use medium grit), then proceed to finer grits, stepping up gradually to 600–800 grit. I recommend using wet/dry sandpaper and sanding in a shallow bowl of water to minimize dust. You can cover a small sponge with the paper. For a satin look, hand-buff on cotton or denim. For a high shine, use a power buffer.

Gluing

Using sealants and glue with polymer clay can be touchy because chemical reactions between products are hard to predict. Spray sealers usually do not work with polymer clay, and your piece will become sticky, though it may take months for a reaction to occur. A hot, humid climate can speed up this reaction.

My recommendations for glues that work with polymer clay include liquid clay, Kato Polyglue, The Ultimate by Crafter's Pick, Aileen's Glue, and Perfect Glue II. Cyanoacrylate is also popular. Sealers and coatings that work with polymer clay include Plaid Polyurethane, Golden Polymer Varnish, and Envirotex Lite. Feel free to experiment with other products. Be sure to test each product on a scrap piece of clay, since some products have ingredients that can also cause the clay to turn sticky with time.

tip

If you still have any small air bubbles trapped in your clay, you can sand them smooth with fine sandpaper.

Jewelry Tools and Techniques

Basic Jewelry Tools

Use **crimping pliers (a)** to compress crimp beads, **wire cutters (b)** to cut wire, **round-nose pliers (c)** to create loops or rings in wire, and **chainnose pliers (d)** to open and close loops and jump rings.

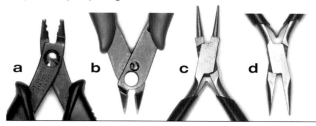

Techniques

To make a basic pendant in this book, determine the desired length of a necklace and add 6 in. (15 cm). Cut a piece of beading wire to that length.

1. String a pendant and beads on the wire in the pattern desired.
2. Add a crimp bead and the desired clasp.
3. String the wire back through the crimp bead and several beads, if appropriate.
4. Crimp the crimp beads and trim excess wire.

Plain loop

1. String beads on wire or a head pin. Trim the wire or head pin ⅜ in. (1 cm) above the top bead. Make a right-angle bend close to the bead.
2. Grab the wire's tip with roundnose pliers. The tip of the wire should be flush with the pliers. Roll the wire to form a half circle. Release the wire.
3. Reposition the pliers in the loop and continue rolling.
4. The finished loop should form a centered circle above the bead.

Opening and closing loops or jump rings

1. Hold the loop or jump ring with two pairs of chainnose pliers as shown.
2. To open the loop or jump ring, bring one pair of pliers toward you and push the other pair away. String materials on the open loop or jump ring. Reverse the steps to close.

Flattened crimp

1. Hold the crimp using the tip of your chainnose pliers. Squeeze the pliers firmly to flatten the crimp.
2. Tug the wire to make sure the crimp has a solid grip. If the wire slides, repeat the steps with a new crimp.

Folded crimp

1. Position the crimp bead in the notch closest to the crimping pliers' handle.
2. Separate the wires and firmly squeeze the crimp.
3. Move the crimp into the notch at the pliers' tip and hold the crimp as shown. Squeeze the crimp bead, folding it in half at the indentation.
4. Test that the folded crimp is secure.

Polymer clay can be shaped in so many ways. You can shape almost anything: simple beads, hearts, and bears to wonderfully delicate flowers, characters, and even sculpture.

Taking a little extra time to get an even shape pays off greatly. Make sure the clay is smooth and there are no air pockets or fingerprints. Create any shape desired in any color you like.

Polymer clay is also ideal for molding. There are many different types of molds on the market, and you can use whichever type you prefer.

The projects in this section are varied, easy, and fun to do. You can create pendants, decorate vases, and even dress up drawer pulls.

Shaped and Molded Clay

Circle Necklace and Earrings

MATERIALS

- Polymer clay:
  Pearl
  Turquoise
  Green
- 10 square crystal beads
- Silver seed beads
- 2 crimp beads
- Toggle clasp
- Beading wire
- 2 2-in. (5 cm) head pins
- 2 ear wires

TOOLS

- Clay machine or acrylic roller
- Silicone roller
- Slicing blade or craft knife
- Needle tool
- Ceramic tile covered with polyester batting
- Roundnose pliers
- Chainnose pliers
- Wire cutters
- Crimping pliers
- Circle cutter set*

*Used in this project: Makin's Clay circle cutter set.

Use pearl clay to create a subtle color variation. (See chatoyant effect, p. 44.)

Begin with this basic necklace-and-earrings set.
You can practice making shapes while combining
clays to make beautiful colors.

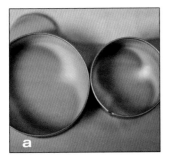

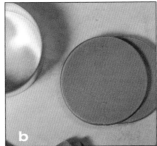

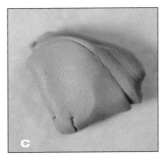

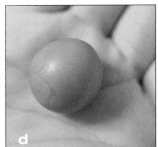

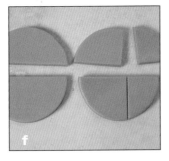

INSTRUCTIONS

1. Condition and completely mix equal parts of turquoise, green, and pearl clay (see p. 6). Create a sheet of clay by running clay through a clay machine on the thickest setting.

2. Use circle cutters to cut out four large circles, twelve medium circles, and four small circles. **(a)**

3. Make a large bead by combining two large circles. **(b)** Press the clay together, fold in half (pressing from the fold to the edges to avoid trapping air), and repeat. **(c)**

4. Roll the clay in your hands, firmly at first to create a ball and then more gently to smooth. **(d)**

5. Flatten the ball slightly. Smooth and shape until you have a round disk **(e)**.

6. Repeat steps 3–5 to make the remaining beads, substituting the following for the two large clay circles:
• one large and one medium circle (make two beads).
• two medium circles (make four beads).
• one medium circle (make two beads).
• one small circle (make two beads).

7. Cut the last two small circles as shown in the photo. **(f)** Repeat steps 3–5 with each of the top three sections to make three beads for one earring. Repeat with the bottom sections for the other earring beads.

8. Use a rubber brayer or silicone roller on all beads to smooth and remove any fingerprints. **(g)**

9. Use a piercing pin or sharp needle tool to create

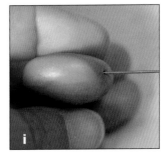

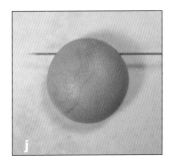

a hole near the top of each bead (center the holes in the earring beads). To keep the hole centered in the bead, control the pin, keeping it even from both the front and back of the bead and along the top of the bead. Twist the piercing pin to drill the hole; don't simply push the pin through the bead. **(h, i)**

10. When the pin appears on the other side of the bead, remove the pin and drill from the other side. **(j)** This will help keep the holes in the bead smooth. Repeat for all of the beads.

11. Bake the beads upside down for one hour. Cool.

12. String the beads on the beading wire, including the cube and seed beads as desired. Add seed beads until you reach the desired length. String a crimp bead and half of the toggle clasp. Go back through the crimp bead and crimp (see p. 10).

13. String a large, medium, and small earring bead on a head pin. Make a plain loop above the beads and attach it to an ear wire (see p. 10). Repeat for the other earring.

Heart Fan Pull

MATERIALS
- Polymer clay:
  White
- Alcohol ink:
  Pink*
  Green*
- Fan pull assembly*

*Used in this project: Ranger Adirondack Alcohol Ink in raisin and pesto, wire heart fan pull from Hobby Lobby.

TOOLS
- Clay machine or acrylic roller
- Silicone roller
- Slicing blade or craft knife
- Needle tool
- Clay shaper
- Ceramic tile covered with polyester batting
- Roundnose pliers
- Chainnose pliers
- Paintbrush
- Plastic card (optional)

*Building on the techniques used for the Circle
Necklace and Earrings, this fan pull is easy and quick.
Make a few to match all the rooms in your house.*

a

b

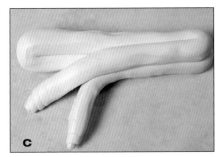

c

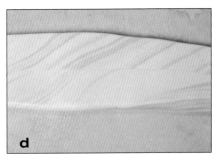

d

e

f

g

h

5. Use an acrylic roller to flatten the clay. Flatten until the piece is about the thickness of the thickest setting on the clay machine. **(d)**

6. Run this sheet through your clay machine. Fold in half and run through the clay machine again. Repeat until you have a nice, swirled pattern. **(e)**

7. Cut a 3-in. (7.6 cm) square from the clay sheet. Fold in half, pressing the air from the fold out to the edge. Repeat, folding the other way. Form this square into a smooth ball of clay. Roll one edge in the palm of your hands to form a teardrop shape. Flatten.

8. Use a plastic card or a paintbrush handle to create the top of the heart. **(f, g)**

9. Use a paintbrush handle or your fingers to smooth the top of the heart. A clay shaper helps define the heart shape. **(h)**

10. Repeat steps 2–6 with green ink. Repeat steps 7–9 with the remaining pink clay and the new green clay to make a total of two pink and one green heart shapes. Check that they will fit stacked on top of each other on the fan pull assembly with at least ½ in. (1.3 cm) of wire remaining.

11. Use a needle tool to make a hole from the top of one heart to the bottom. Enlarge the hole with a larger needle tool. Repeat with the remaining hearts.

12. Bake the hearts for one hour. Cool.

13. String the hearts on the fan pull assembly. If the holes are too small, use a drill bit to enlarge them (see p. 9).

14. Attach the fan pull assembly to the ball chain with a plain loop (see p. 10).

INSTRUCTIONS

1. Condition the white polymer clay (see p. 6). Run it through the clay machine on a medium setting to make a clay sheet. Cut the sheet in half.

2. Place 5–7 drops of pink alcohol ink on half of the sheet, and brush to thin and help it dry. **(a)**

3. Starting on one edge, tightly roll the clay sheet to form a log of clay. Press as much air out as possible as you roll. **(b)**

4. Roll the log, twisting and stretching as you roll. Fold the log in half, and then fold it in half again. **(c)**

Enhanced Heart Necklace

MATERIALS
- Polymer clay:
  Pearl
  White
  Violet
  Silver (small amount)
- 3 in. (7.6 cm) twisted silver wire
- 2 in. (5 cm) silver wire
- 10–20 heat-set stones or crystals
- 2 mm buna or rubber cord, desired length
- O-ring
- 2 ear wires
- Instant tacky glue

TOOLS
- Clay machine or acrylic roller
- Silicone roller
- Slicing blade or craft knife
- Clay shaper
- Ceramic tile covered with polyester batting
- Roundnose pliers
- Chainnose pliers
- Wire cutters

Just adding a wire element and crystals can completely change the look of a project. Many different items can be used with polymer clay—as long as they can take the heat!

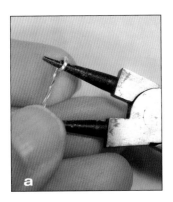

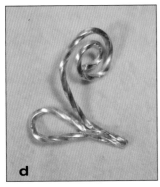

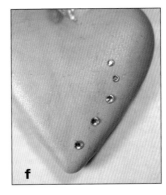

INSTRUCTIONS

1. Condition and completely mix pearl, white, violet, and a small amount of silver clay as desired to create a pleasing color (see p. 6).

2. Form a pendant-sized heart, following steps 3–9 on p. 15.

3. Wrap one end of the twisted wire around the tip of your roundnose pliers. **(a)**

4. Use pliers to make a loose coil with about 1 in. (2.5 cm) of twisted wire. **(b)**

5. Make a loop on the other end of the wire large enough for the cord to pass through. **(c)**

6. Bend the wire back on itself about ½ in. (1.3 cm) below the loop. **(d)**

7. Press the bent portion of wire into the top of the heart firmly. (Leave the coil up for now.) **(e)**

8. Place the heat-set crystals face up on one side of the heart in any pattern you like. **(f)**

9. With two pea-sized pieces of clay, form two small cone-shaped pieces for the cord ends. Pierce a hole in the flat end of the cone with a needle tool, going about halfway through the cone. Repeat for the other cone.

10. Use a smaller portion of blended clay to make an earring heart. Make a plain loop with 1 in. (2.5 cm) of silver wire (see p. 10), twist the end, and then push the wire into the top of the heart. Repeat to make a second heart.

11. Bake all hearts for one hour. Cool. Bend the coiled wire against the front of the heart as shown in the main photo of the pendant.

12. If necessary, enlarge the hole in the cone ends so the cord will fit. String the pendant on the cord. Pass both ends of the cord through the O-ring in opposite directions. Glue a cone to each end of the cord. Let dry. **(g)**

13. Open the ear wire loops and attach the small hearts.

Molded Drawer Pull

MATERIALS
- Polymer clay:
  Black
  Copper
- Powdered pigment:
  Gold*
- Ceramic or metal
  drawer pull

*Used in this project: Pearl-Ex
Powdered Pigments by Jacquard
in Aztec Gold.*

TOOLS
- Clay machine or acrylic
  roller
- Silicone roller
- Slicing blade or craft
  knife
- Ceramic tile covered with
  polyester batting
- Art mold to fit your
  drawer pull*
- Fine paintbrush

*Used in this project: Krafty Lady Art
Molds, AM149 Clover.*

Update old dressers with a fresh new look by adding your own touch to drawer pulls. This project uses a ceramic drawer pull bought at a craft store to make an elegant statement.

INSTRUCTIONS

1. Condition the black polymer clay and run it through the clay machine on a thin setting (see p. 6). Condition the copper clay on the same setting, and set aside.

2. Cover the drawer pull with a sheet of black polymer clay, pressing the excess clay toward the end of the pull. **(a)**

3. Smooth the excess clay, using firm pressure. **(b)** Trim the excess clay with a craft knife. Repeat if necessary.

4. Press the copper clay into the art mold (see p. 8). If desired, use a fine paintbrush to add powder pigment highlights. **(c)**

5. Place the molded piece on the covered drawer pull. Press the clay pieces together firmly, being careful not to distort the molded shape. **(d)**

6. Bake for one hour and cool. Attach the pull to a drawer.

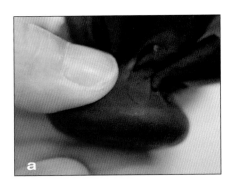

tip

If you are not happy with an item before baking, reform it, reshape it, try using a new mold, or add the extra clay to your scrap bucket.

Exquisite Flower Vase

MATERIALS
- Polymer clay:
  Pearl, 2–3 blocks
  Gold
- 9-in. (23 cm) glass vase

TOOLS
- Clay machine or acrylic roller
- Silicone roller
- Slicing blade or craft knife
- Needle tool
- Clay shaper
- Ceramic tile covered with polyester batting
- Assorted art molds*
- Lint-free towel
- Plastic wrap (optional)
- Hot pad

*Used in this project: Krafty Lady AM337 Three Leaves, AM011 Medium Leaf, AM269 Ivy Leaf, AM255 Skeletal Leaf, AM266 Lg. Geranium Leaf, AM352 Two Frangipani, AM149 Lg. Clover, AM157 Daisy #1, and AM280 Mini Daisy.

tip

If the clay sticks to your fingers as you mold it, cover the clay with plastic wrap, or mist with water.

This project uses nine art molds to create a nice, varied pattern. If you choose a different brand of mold, be sure to use a release agent (see p. 8).

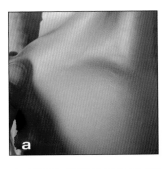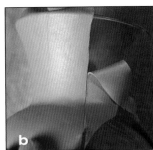

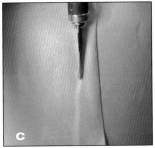

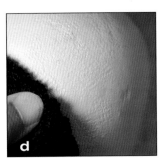

INSTRUCTIONS

1. Condition and completely mix the pearl clay with 1/8 block of gold clay (see p. 6). Add more gold, if desired. Cut the clay in half, and then run half through the clay machine at the #7 setting. Cut a piece as wide as you can, slightly longer than the vase is high.

2. Place that strip lengthwise on the vase. Stretch the clay slightly over the largest part of the vase. **(a)**

3. Smooth the clay sheet to the side of the vase. Press out any air bubbles.

4. Trim the edges of the sheet with a craft knife and remove the excess clay. **(b)**

5. Place another sheet on the vase, overlapping the clay edges slightly. Press gently to the other sheet to see the overlap. Trim the excess clay with a craft knife. **(c)**

6. Smooth the seam with your fingers.

7. Repeat steps 5 and 6 with a third sheet of clay if necessary. Check to be sure the seams are smooth and there are no air pockets.

8. Texture the clay with a lint-free towel by gently pressing the towel to the vase. **(d)**

9. Press a small piece of clay into a mold. You don't have to fill the mold completely; for this project, a thin molded piece works better. Remove the shape, and repeat with the rest of the molds to make the desired number of molded pieces. **(e)**

10. Place the leaves and flowers on the widest area of the vase, overlapping the shapes to cover the front as desired. Add flowers and leaves up the curve of the vase until you have covered the upper half of the vase. **(f)**

11. Lay the vase on its side and bake for one hour. Check for air bubbles while the vase is still warm, and gently press them out with a hot pad or prick with a needle tool and then press. Let cool.

Note: I used two different-sized vases for these photos. Choose any size vase you like.

tip

Texturing the clay helps remove and hide air bubbles. If you do find air bubbles, pick them out with a sharp needle before baking so they don't show up in your finished piece.

Shaped and Molded Clay

Molded Cameo

MATERIALS
- Polymer clay:
  Pearl
  Red
  Yellow
- Gold rectangular metal pendant*
- 5 mm gold-filled jump ring
- Gold cable wire necklace*

Used in this project: Artistrywear by Plaid.

TOOLS
- Clay machine or acrylic roller
- Slicing blade or craft knife
- Needle tool
- Clay shaper
- Ceramic tile covered with polyester batting
- Plastic wrap
- Cameo art mold*

Used in this project: Krafty Lady AM074 Cameo.

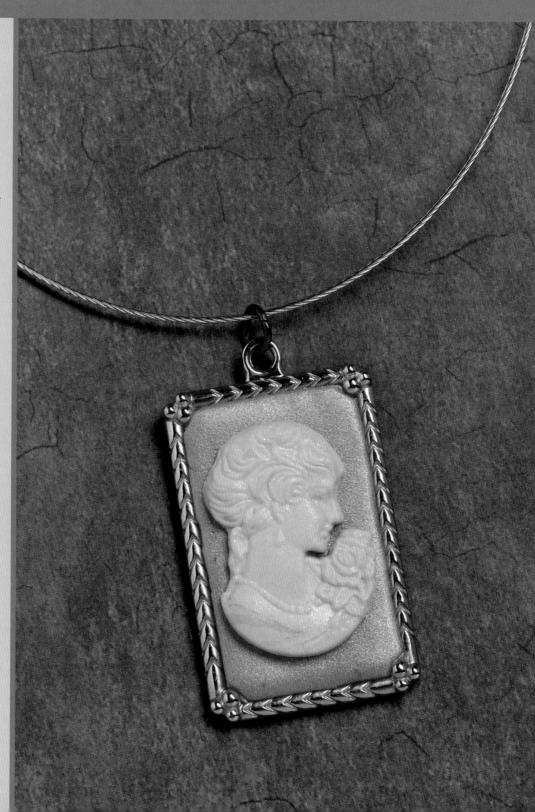

This cameo is just one example of a molded pendant. Use any type of mold to create a customized pendant in colors you love. Make a whole collection to match your style!

a

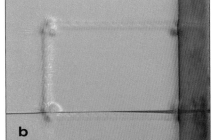

b

c

d

e

f

INSTRUCTIONS

1. Condition the pearl clay (see p. 6). Cut the sheet in half and add a pinch of red and yellow clay to one half. Mix completely. Add more red and yellow, if desired, to get a nice peach color.

2. Run the peach clay through the clay machine on a medium setting. Lay the clay sheet on a ceramic tile. Cover the clay with plastic wrap, and then press the metal pendant face down onto the clay. **(a)**

3. Remove the metal frame and plastic wrap, and cut around the marked line. Remove the excess clay. **(b)**

4. To lift the clay, run the slicing blade under the clay and place it in the metal pendant form, taking care to not trap any air under the clay. Smooth the edges with a clay shaper. **(c)**

5. Pinch off a small amount of conditioned pearl clay. Fill the cameo mold with clay. **(d)**

6. A high part under the cameo's chin can be opened by removing clay with a needle tool. **(e)**

7. Remove the cameo from the mold. Smooth any jagged clay with a needle tool if necessary. **(f)**

8. Center the cameo in the rectangular metal frame. Press the cameo to the peach clay gently.

9. Bake for 30 minutes. Cool.

10. Use a jump ring to hang the pendant on a cable wire necklace (see p. 10).

Molded Mother and Child

MATERIALS

- Polymer clay: Silver
- Liquid polymer clay
- Powdered pigment: Silver*
- 1 in. (2.5 cm) silver twisted wire
- 2 mm buna or rubber cord
- Instant tacky glue*

*Used in this project: Silver Pearl-Ex Powder and Crafter's Pick Ultimate Tacky glue.

TOOLS

- Clay machine or acrylic roller
- Slicing blade
- Craft knife
- Ceramic tile covered with polyester batting
- Roundnose pliers
- Chainnose pliers
- Wire cutters
- Art mold*
- Oval paper punch
- $\frac{5}{64}$-in. (2 mm) drill bit

*Used in this project: Krafty Lady AM096 Madonna art mold.

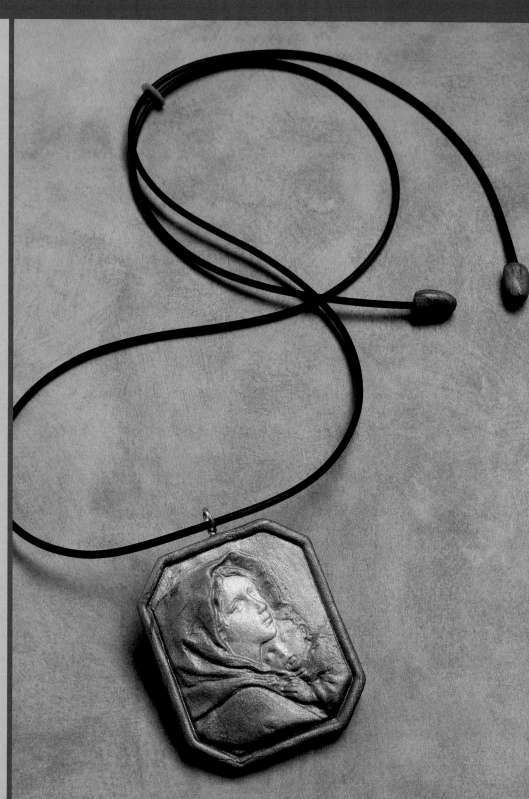

This is one of the easiest projects in the book. It makes a great gift for a new mom or for Mother's Day. You will learn how to create a buna cord separator, but you can use an O-ring or just hang the pendant on a purchased chain, if you like.

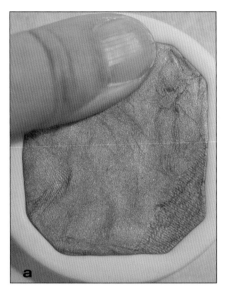

a

INSTRUCTIONS

1. Condition the silver clay (see p. 6).

2. Press a medium-sized ball of silver clay into a mold. Press firmly to get a good impression. If there is too much clay, remove some of the excess. If there is not enough, add a little. **(a)**

3. To remove the clay from the mold, press your finger in the center and gently pull up on the edges. **(b)**

4. Check to be sure you have a good image. If not, roll the clay in your hands and repeat steps 2 and 3.

5. Center the silver wire on the roundnose pliers and bend the wire around the pliers' jaws. **(c)**

6. Pinch the wire with chainnose pliers to form a loop. **(d)**

7. Bend the ends of the wire 45 degrees away from the circle. **(e)**

8. Run the remaining silver clay through the clay machine at the thickest setting to form a sheet. Cut one edge straight with the slicing blade. Place the wire ends overlapping the straight edge, with the loop extending past the edge. **(f)**

b

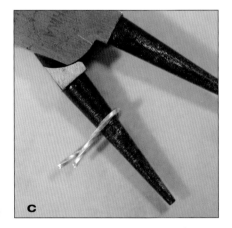

c

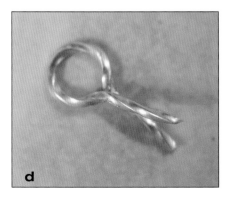

d

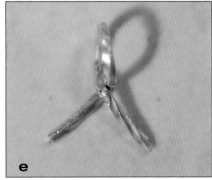

e

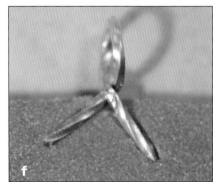

f

9. Place the molded piece on the clay sheet, face up, with the tops aligned. Press the mold and the clay sheet together gently. Trim around the molded piece with a slicing blade. **(g, h)**

10. Check that the edges are smooth. Use a clay tool to smooth, if necessary.

11. With two pea-sized pieces of clay, form two small cone-shaped pieces for the cord ends. Pierce a hole in the flat end of the cone, going about halfway through the cone. Repeat for the other cone.

12. Bake all three pieces for 30 minutes. Cool.

13. Mix half a teaspoon of powder pigment into a small amount of liquid clay directly on a ceramic tile. The powder will thicken the liquid clay. Be careful not to use too much powder or the sheet could crumble when you drill it. **(i)**

14. Bake for 20 minutes and let the clay sheet cool.

15. Use the oval paper punch to punch an oval from the clay sheet. (If you don't have an oval punch, you can cut a rectangle with a craft knife instead.) **(j)**

16. Use the drill bit to make two holes in the oval. This oval separator will allow you to adjust the length of the necklace. **(k)**

17. String the pendant on the cord.

18. Trim the cord ends at an angle, then thread each end through a hole in the oval separator, going in opposite directions. **(l)**

19. Glue the cones on the ends of the cord to finish the necklace.

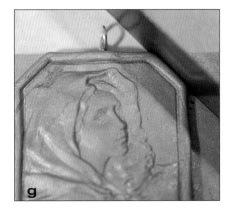

g

h

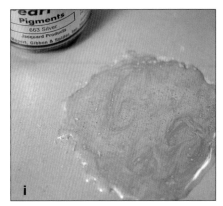

i

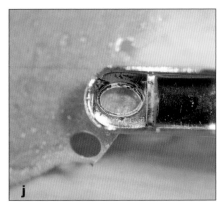

j

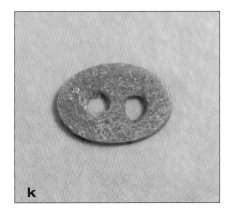

k

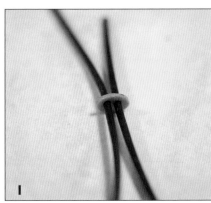

l

More Inspirational Ideas

I used a cookie press misted with water to mold this apple. I painted the shape with stencil paint and used metallic silver clay to make a chatoyant effect. For more information about creating a chatoyant effect, see Chapter 3.

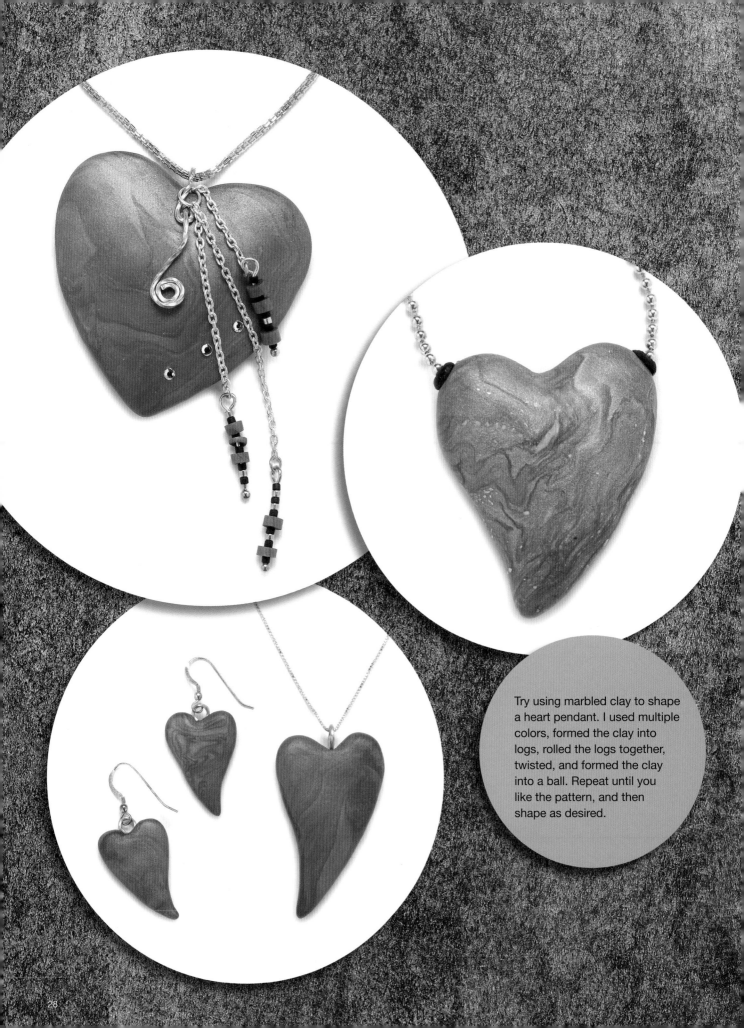

Try using marbled clay to shape a heart pendant. I used multiple colors, formed the clay into logs, rolled the logs together, twisted, and formed the clay into a ball. Repeat until you like the pattern, and then shape as desired.

Cookie-type cutters are great with polymer clay. They make it easy to cut perfect shapes every time. Paper punches also work well with polymer clay; use them on both raw clay and very thin sheets of baked clay.

To make exquisite textures on clay, stamps are ideal. You can use just about any type of rubber or acrylic stamp to make detailed patterns. Liquid clay also offers a different way to create smooth, thin layers.

Experiment with the different tools and techniques in this chapter to create the perfect necklace or home décor item.

Cutters, Punches, Stamps, and Liquid Clay

Cut Flower Pin

MATERIALS
- Polymer clay:
  Pearl
  White
- Chalk*:
  Pink
  Gold
- Liquid polymer clay
- Pin back

*Used in this project: Craft-T products classic "glimmer" chalks.

TOOLS
- Clay machine or acrylic roller
- Slicing blade or craft knife
- Ceramic tile covered with polyester batting
- Any color pigment stamp pad
- Cutters*
  2-in. (5 cm) circle
  ¾-in. (1.9 cm) circle
  1¼-in. (3.2 cm) teardrop
  ⅞-in. (2.2 cm) teardrop
- Makeup sponge cut into quarters
- Small, shallow glass bowl

*Used in this project: Makin's Clay Cutters.

tip

Instead of chalks, you can use old eye shadow or blush.

Using simple cookie cutters, create a fun and easy flower pin for your next garden party.

INSTRUCTIONS

1. Condition and mix completely equal halves pearl and white clay (see p. 6). Run the clay through the clay machine at a medium setting to make a sheet.

2. Cut one 2-in. (5 cm) circle from the sheet. Ink a ¾-in. (1.9 cm) circle cutter and stamp it in the center of the clay circle. Make an ink dot in the center of that circle. **(a)**

3. Cut 19 large petals using a 1¼-in. (3.2 cm) teardrop cutter. Cut six petals using a small ⅞-in. (2.2 cm) teardrop cutter. **(b)**

4. Rub one corner of the makeup sponge in pink chalk, and brush chalk on the petals. **(c)**

5. Pinch the round end of each petal. **(d)**

6. Place a large petal on the clay circle, with its point on the marked circle, aimed toward the center dot. Place another petal next to the previous one. Repeat to finish the outside circle. **(e)**

7. Place a large petal with its point touching the dot in the center of the circle; center the pinched portion of the petal between the petals on the outside circle. Place another petal next to the previous petal (the petals may overlap). Repeat to finish the middle circle. **(f)**

8. Repeat step 7 with small petals to finish the inside circle. **(g)**

9. Form a small amount of clay into a slightly flattened ball, powder with gold chalk, and place the ball in the center of the flower. **(h)**

10. Bake the flower face down for one hour. Remove from the oven and place into a small bowl while still warm, face up, to bend the outside petals up slightly.

11. When cool, brush a small amount of liquid clay on the back of the flower, and place a pin back on the liquid. Cut a strip of clay the width of the pin base and 1 in. (2.5 cm) long. Place this over the pin base and press to adhere.

12. Bake for 15 minutes and cool.

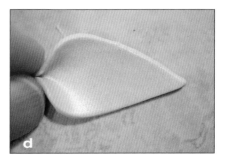

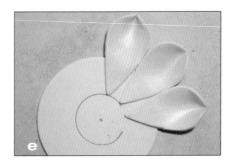

Punched Flower Tin

MATERIALS
- Polymer clay:
  Black
  Pearl
  White
- Alcohol ink*
- Small mint tin

Used in this project: Ranger Adirondack Alcohol Ink.

TOOLS
- Clay machine or acrylic roller
- Slicing blade or craft knife
- Needle tool
- Clay shaper
- Ball stylus
- Ceramic tile covered with polyester batting
- Paper punches (guards removed):
  Teardrop
  1/8-in. (3 mm) circle
  Small flower
- Towel (optional)
- Leaf stamp (optional)

Creating covered tins is easier than it looks. You can decorate these lovely tins using simple paper punches for an exquisite, textured look.

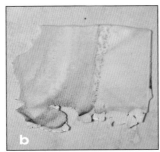

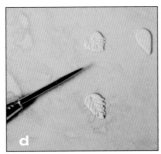

INSTRUCTIONS

1. Condition black clay and run through the clay machine at a medium setting (see p. 6).

2. Cover the top of the tin, taking care to press out any trapped air. Press down on the sides, then the corner to work out the excess clay. **(a)**

3. Trim the excess clay. Texture with a towel, if desired.

4. Condition and mix white and pearl clay together. Cut the clay into 5–8 pieces.

5. Place a few drops of one of the inks on one piece of clay. (Use more if you want a more intense color.) Let the ink dry, then fold the sheet in half, run through the clay machine, and repeat until you have a nice mix, turning as desired. Run the sheet through the clay machine at the thinnest setting. Repeat with the other colors. **(b)**

6. Place the clay sheet in the paper punch, and punch out the flowers, petals, and leaves. **(c)**

7. Use a needle tool to draw veins in the leaves, or press a punched clay shape onto a leaf stamp to make veins. **(d, e)**

8. Place the flowers and leaves on the tin cover as desired. **(f)** Press a ball stylus into the center of the circles and small flowers to add dimension.

9. Continue adding leaves and flowers until you are happy with the look. **(g)**

10. Bake the top for one hour, cool, and place it back on the tin. Run the remaining black clay through the clay machine at a medium setting to create a sheet of clay.

11. Trim one long side of the sheet straight to make a strip. With the top on the tin, lay the straight edge along the top and around the can. Cut the excess where the strips meet. Smooth the seam. Trim the clay at the bottom of the tin.

12. Remove the tin top, and thin the clay where the top was by gently pressing the clay up. Trim any excess clay. Place the top back on to check that the tin is covered and the top fits.

13. Remove the top and bake the tin bottom for one hour. Cool.

Delicate Flowers Pendant

MATERIALS
- Polymer clay:
  Pearl
  White
- Powdered pigment in various colors*
- 5 mm gold-filled jump ring
- Gold cable necklace

*Used in this project: Pearl-Ex powdered pigments by Jacquard.

TOOLS
- Clay machine or acrylic roller
- Silicone roller
- Slicing blade or craft knife
- Ball stylus
- Ceramic tile covered with polyester batting
- Roundnose pliers
- Chainnose pliers
- Wire cutters
- Crimping pliers
- Paper punches (guards removed)
  Teardrop
  ⅛-in. (3 mm) circle
  Flower
- Round cookie cutter
- Plastic wrap

This delicate flowered pendant is easy to make with ordinary paper punches. You can use this technique to dress up just about any flat surface.

INSTRUCTIONS

1. Condition and completely mix pearl and white clay together (see p. 6). Run through the clay machine at the thickest setting.

2. Cut the sheet in half and stack the two halves. Cover with plastic wrap. Use a round cookie cutter to cut a circle. (The plastic wrap will give you a nice, rounded edge.) **(a)**

3. Run the excess clay through the clay machine at the #5 setting. Decide how many colors you will use for the flowers and leaves, and cut the clay into that number of pieces.

4. Brush one of the pigments on one piece of clay. Fold the sheet in half and run it through the clay machine. Repeat until the clay is thoroughly mixed. Run the sheet through the clay machine at a thin setting. Repeat with the other pigment colors.

5. Place a clay sheet in the paper punch and punch out an assortment of flowers, petals, and leaves. Repeat for the remaining clay colors. **(b)**

6. Use the needle tool to create veins in the leaves. (You can also use a stamp—see p. 33, step 7.) **(c)**

7. Place the flowers and leaves on the pendant as desired. **(d)**

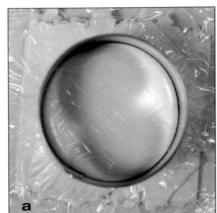

a

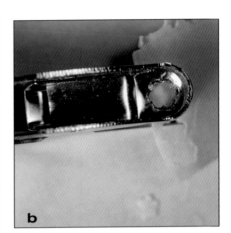

b

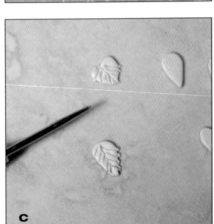

c

d

8. Use a ball stylus to impress the flowers; attach the pieces firmly, but don't flatten them too much. **(e)** Using a needle tool, pierce a hole near the center top of the pendant.

9. Bake the pendant for 30 minutes and cool.

10. Thread a jump ring through the pendant's hole, and slide the jump ring on the gold cable necklace.

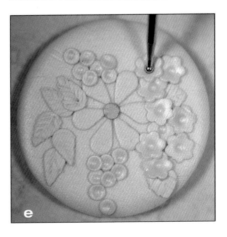

e

tip

To prevent darkening while baking, wrap white or translucent clay pieces in polyester batting.

Stamped Vase

MATERIALS
- Polymer clay:
  Pearl
  White
  Red (very small amount)
- Glass vase

TOOLS
- Clay machine or acrylic roller
- Silicone roller
- Slicing blade or craft knife
- Needle tool
- Ceramic tile covered with polyester batting
- Rolling stamp wheel*
- Optional: Clay extruder*
- 1-in. (2.5 cm) diameter rubber tubing
- Length of strong wire
- Hot pad

*Used in this project: Clearsnap Rollagraph Stamp Wheel, Pebbles, and Makin's Clay Professional Ultimate Clay Extruder.

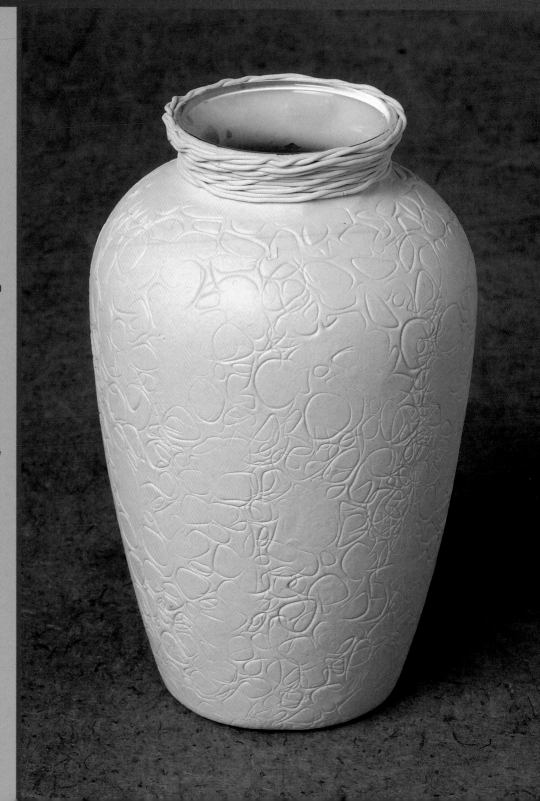

Covering glass vases is a great way to create unique items that add color to a room. This project offers tips for covering a tapered vase smoothly—all you need is a little patience.

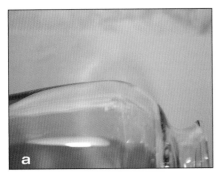

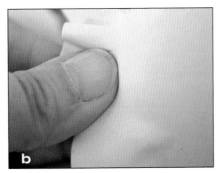

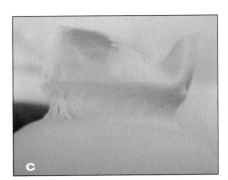

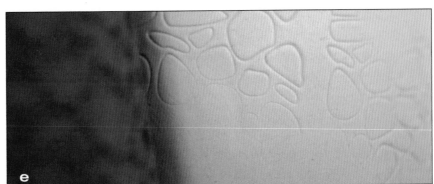

INSTRUCTIONS

1. Condition and completely mix the white, pearl, and red clay together (see p. 6). Run a sheet through the clay machine at the thinnest setting.

2. Trim one edge straight and lay the vase on the clay. **(a)**

3. Wrap the sheet of clay around the thickest area of the vase, stretching the clay slightly to fit. **(b)**

4. Gently press the clay where the edges meet.

5. Starting at the thickest area, gently work the excess clay down the vase by alternately pressing the clay down and pulling gently on the edge of the clay.

6. Continue in this manner until you reach the bottom of the vase. Smooth the clay over the edge of the base. Trim the excess clay at the base.

7. Work the excess clay up the vase as in step 6. Work the clay over the top edge. **(c)**

8. At the neck of the vase, you will have some clay overlap. A piece of rubber tubing with a length of wire inside helps to smooth those areas. Roll the tubing where the clay is overlapped toward the top of the vase. Trim the excess clay at the top of the vase. **(d)**

9. Use a rolling stamp wheel to texture the clay. **(e)**

10. Bake the vase for one hour. Check to be sure there are no trapped air bubbles. If there are, use a hot pad and press the air out. If necessary, prick any air bubbles with a needle tool.

tip

When using the roller to texture the vase, you might accidentally mark the lip of the vase with the roller. I didn't notice that the lip of my vase was marked until after baking (it goes to show that we all make mistakes!). If that happens to you, try using this technique to hide any trouble spots.

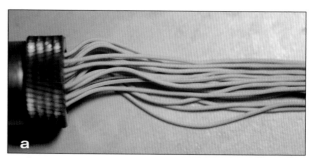

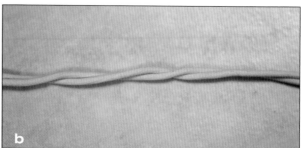

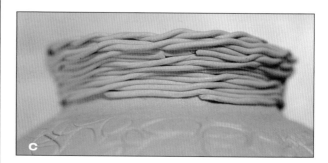

1. Recondition the excess clay, roll it into a thick snake, and place it in an extruder. Use the #8 disc to extrude the clay. **(a)**

2. Take two extruded noodles and twist them together. **(b)**

3. Place the twisted noodles on the vase around the neck. Continue adding noodles until you reach the top of the vase. **(c)**

4. Bake again for one hour.

Liquid Clay Heart Pendant and Earrings

MATERIALS
- Liquid clay
- Powdered pigments*:
  Gold
  Red
- Metal heart pendant*
- Finished gold chain
  necklace*
- 15 in. (38 cm) gold-link
  chain
- 16 gold jump rings
- 2 gold ear wires

*Used in this project: Pearl-Ex
Powdered Pigments by Jacquard in
Aztec Gold and Super Russet; Gold
Artistrywear Accessories—Metal
Pendants: Heart; and Plaid gold chain.

TOOLS
- Clay machine or acrylic
  roller
- Silicone roller
- Slicing blade or craft
  knife
- Needle tool
- Ceramic tile
- Roundnose pliers
- Chainnose pliers
- Wire cutters
- Paint palette
- Fine paintbrush
- Toothpick
- Heart punch*

*Used in this project: EK Success
punch.

Liquid clay is versatile and mixes with many other products. You can add powdered pigment to make just about any color in the rainbow! For a variation on this technique, try using alcohol inks; they will create a more transparent look.

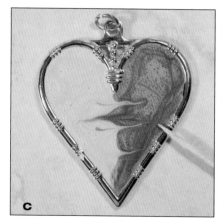

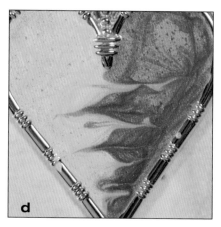

tip

Liquid clay will stick to glass—try cutting various shapes from baked liquid clay to dress up a vase that you can change with the seasons, or make thin window clings.

INSTRUCTIONS

1. Fill two wells of a paint palette with liquid clay. Add gold powdered pigment to one well and red powdered pigment to the other. Mix the powder into the clay with a toothpick. **(a)**

2. Use a small paintbrush to fill half of the heart with the gold mix and the other half with the red mix. **(b)**

3. Allow the clay to settle, and prick any air bubbles that appear. Use a toothpick to drag a line of red clay into the gold half. **(c)**

4. Drag the gold clay into the red half using a clean toothpick or the other end of the toothpick.

5. Wipe the toothpick if necessary, and repeat steps 3 and 4 a few times, continuing down the heart. **(d)**

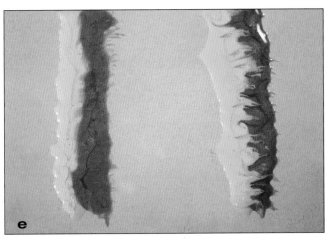

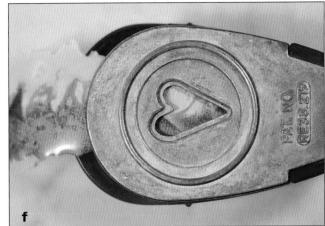

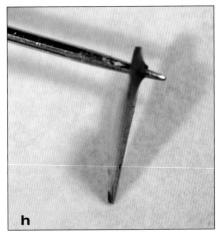

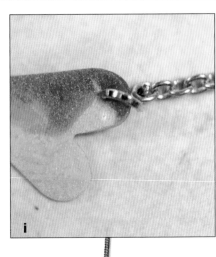

6. Brush a stripe of gold liquid on a ceramic tile, and brush a stripe of red next to the gold. Drag the colors as above. Repeat for a second stripe. **(e)**

7. Bake the pendant and the liquid clay strips for 20 minutes. Cool on the tile.

8. Thread the pendant on a finished chain to complete the necklace.

9. Turn the heart punch over, and center the heart between the gold and red stripes. Punch five hearts with red on the right side, and punch five hearts with gold on the right side. (My heart punch has one raised side.) **(f)**

10. Place one heart on a ceramic tile. Using a needle tool, make a hole in the top of one side of the heart. Take care not to make the hole too close to the edge. **(g)**

11. Pick up the heart and press it onto the needle tool to make a complete hole. **(h)**

12. Cut a 15-in. (38 cm) chain into six 2½-in. (6.4 cm) lengths. Open a jump ring, and attach a heart and one end link of chain. Place a jump ring on the other end of the chain. **(i)**

13. Place hearts on both ends of two more pieces of chain in the same way. Place jump rings near the middle of these two chains so the hearts hang randomly.

14. Attach the jump rings to an ear wire (see p. 10). Repeat for the second earring.

More Inspirational Ideas

Create a frame with a double thickness of baked clay covered with black clay. I sprinkled the frame with small, white punched snowflakes and added a large stencil-cut snowflake at the top left corner.

Use translucent clay to make a stunning pendant.

FUN CRACKLE TECHNIQUE

To create a crackle finish on your clay, run a sheet of clay through a clay machine at the thickest setting, and place the sheet on a ceramic tile. Using a heat gun, heat the top of the clay until the clay surface turns dull. (Do not overheat, or you will bake the sheet.) Immediately run the slicing blade under the sheet to remove it from the tile. Reduce the thickness setting on the clay machine by one, and run the sheet through. Reduce by one again, turn the sheet 90 degrees, and run the sheet through. Repeat without turning. This process will create a crackled clay sheet. Try using powders, acrylic paints, or a stamp pad to accent the crackle. Cut shapes if desired, or add crackled clay to a finished object. The crackled sheet will need to be baked so it doesn't fall apart.

The tin shown above is made from a thin sheet, which created a fine crackle. Only the top was covered because a crackled sheet will not bend.

To make a pendant, brush the top of the clay with a small amount of pigment, cut into the shape desired, and place on an uncured sheet of clay. Pierce and bake.

Cover a vase with white or cream-colored clay and add punched flowers as desired.

One of the best tools developed for polymer clay is an extruder. An extruder creates even snakes of clay without having to roll them by hand, which takes some practice. There are several different types of extruders.

Metallic polymer clay contains mica particles. Mica particles aren't spherical, so when the clay goes through the clay machine, the mica is aligned in one direction. This creates a mica shift, or chatoyant effect. The top of the sheet is a lighter color than the edge, and the color will look different when viewed at different angles. Reconditioning the clay realigns the mica particles again to allow you to try a different technique.

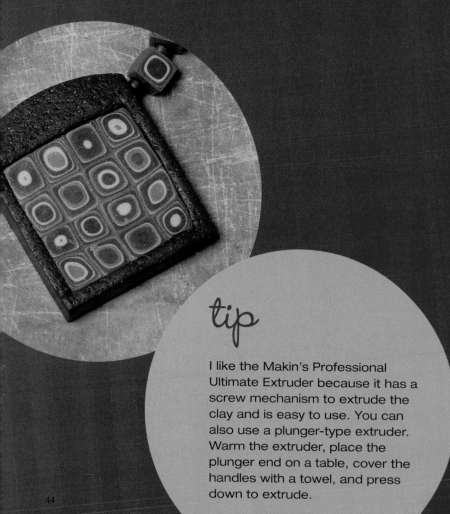

Extrusion, Chatoyant, and Mosaic Effects

tip

I like the Makin's Professional Ultimate Extruder because it has a screw mechanism to extrude the clay and is easy to use. You can also use a plunger-type extruder. Warm the extruder, place the plunger end on a table, cover the handles with a towel, and press down to extrude.

Lavender Recycled Container

MATERIALS
- Polymer clay: White
- Artist pan pastel: Violet*
- Glass container

*Used in this project: Pan Pastel by Colorfin.

TOOLS
- Clay machine or acrylic roller
- Silicone roller
- Slicing blade or craft knife
- Needle tool
- Ceramic tile covered with polyester batting
- Clay extruder*
- Mop brush
- Nylon scouring pad

*Used in this project: Makin's Clay Professional Ultimate Clay Extruder.

tip

Kato clay does not usually stick to itself unless pressed together. If you are using a different clay, be extra careful during step 5.

This is a fun way to reuse a glass candle container when the candle is gone. Be sure to remove any remaining wax and wash the container before using.

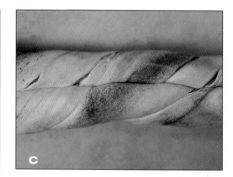

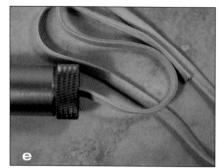

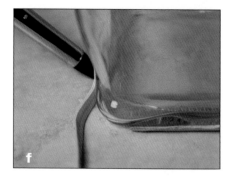

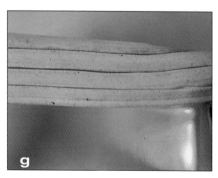

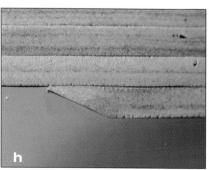

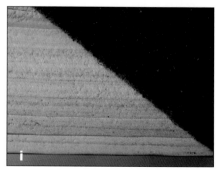

INSTRUCTIONS

1. Condition the white clay (see p. 6). Run a sheet through the clay machine at a medium setting.

2. Lay the clay sheet on a ceramic tile and use a mop brush to dab pastel pigment on the sheet, or press clay to the pastel container. **(a)**

3. Starting on one edge, roll the clay into a thick snake. Roll and twist the snake, fold the snake into quarters, and repeat. **(b, c)**

4. Stop when the pastel color is visible on the outside of the snake. Roll the clay into a snake that will fit into the extruder. Place the clay in the extruder, cutting off any excess. Place the #11 disc on the barrel and then the end. Insert the plunger into the other end of the barrel. **(d)**

5. Twist the handle to extrude the clay. Repeat until you have extruded all of the clay. **(e)**

6. Cut the end of the clay strip at an angle, and then press it to the bottom of the glass container. **(f)**

7. Press the strip around the container, following the lines of the clay added previously. Continue spiraling the strips until the container is completely covered. **(g)**

8. When one strip is completely used, cut the end at an angle. Cut a second strip the same way, match the angles, and continue up the glass. **(h)**

9. When the container is covered, press a scouring pad on the clay to seal the strips together and add texture. **(i)**

10. Cover the lid with clay in the same way.

11. Place the container and the lid on its side on a ceramic tile. Bake for one hour and cool.

Tube Bead Necklace

MATERIALS
- Polymer clay:
  Turquoise
  Green
  White or pearl
- Beading wire
- 6 crimp tubes
- Lobster claw clasp
- Soldered jump ring
- Glass seed beads

TOOLS
- Clay machine or acrylic roller
- Slicing blade or craft knife
- Ceramic tile covered with polyester batting
- Roundnose pliers
- Chainnose pliers
- Wire cutters
- Clay extruder and 1 mm extruder adaptor*
- Glass cutting mat*
- Optional: Heating pad

*Used in this project: Makin's Clay Professional Ultimate Clay Extruder and 1 mm Makin's Professional ClayCore, Walnut Hollow glass cutting mat.

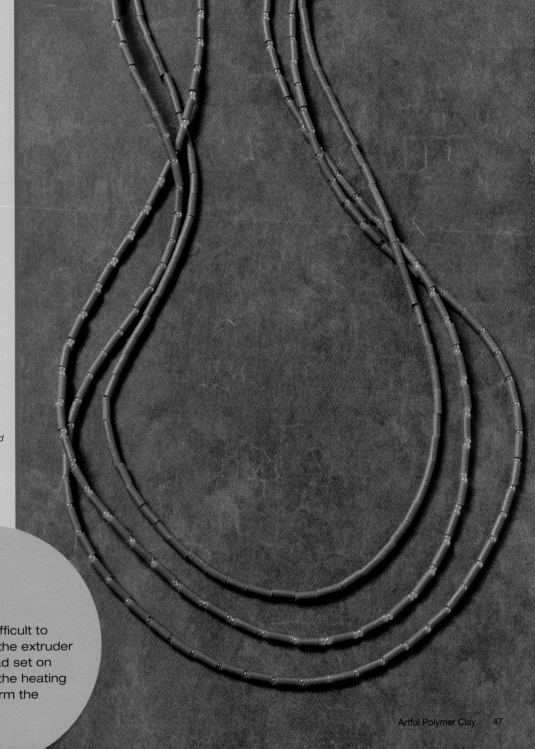

tip

If your clay is difficult to extrude, place the extruder on a heating pad set on warm and fold the heating pad over to warm the extruder.

Use an extruder adaptor to make hollow tube beads, and create a slender necklace perfect for a sunny summer day. Make the strands as long (or as short) as you want.

INSTRUCTIONS

1. Condition and completely mix equal parts turquoise, green, and pearl clay (see p. 6). Run a sheet through the clay machine at the thickest setting.

2. Roll the clay into a thick snake and place it in the extruder. **(a)**

3. Place the 1 mm extruder adaptor on the extruder with the #2 single-hole disc, and add the end cap. Twist the handle until the clay just starts to extrude. **(b)**

4. Check that the adaptor is centered in the clay. Adjust if necessary. **(c)**

5. Extrude the clay. **(d)**

6. Cut the extruded clay into lengths the width of the ceramic tile. Cover the tile with batting and place the clay on top.

7. Bake for one hour. Cool.

8. Trim the ends off all the strips. (When the clay is cut while soft, the hole gets pinched closed.) Place the strips of clay on a cutting mat with ¼-in. (6 mm) markings. Using a craft knife or a slicing blade, cut the strips in ¼-in. (6 mm) pieces. **(e)**

9. Determine the desired length of your necklace and add 6 in. (15 cm). Cut a piece of beading wire that length, and cut two more pieces a few inches shorter (see tip). Put a small binder clip on one end of a wire, then string on the clay beads and glass beads in the desired pattern. **(f)**

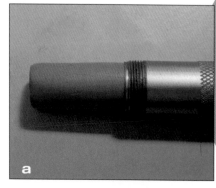
a

tip

The example has one strand with clay beads only, one with alternating clay and glass beads, and one with a pattern of one clay bead and two glass beads. Make the three strands slightly different lengths for a staggered drape.

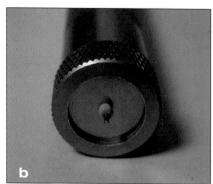
b

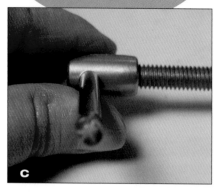
c

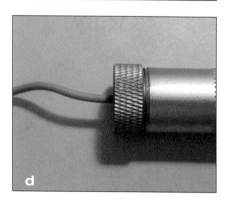
d

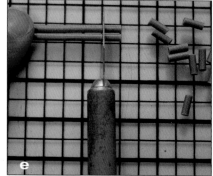
e

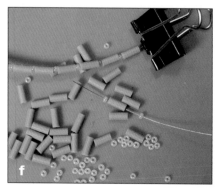
f

10. String a crimp bead and clasp over all three of wires on one end, and string a crimp bead and a jump ring on the other end. Crimp the crimp beads (see p. 10).

Metallic Tube Bead Necklace

MATERIALS

- Polymer clay: Black
- Powdered pigments in various colors*
- Beading wire
- 2 crimp beads for each strand
- 2 split rings for each strand
- S-hook

*Used in this project: Pearl-Ex Powdered Pigments by Jacquard, EZ-Crimps.

TOOLS

- Clay machine or acrylic roller
- Silicone roller
- Slicing blade or craft knife
- Ceramic tile covered with polyester batting
- Roundnose pliers
- Chainnose pliers
- Wire cutters
- Clay extruder
- Scrap paper
- Mop brush
- Glass cutting mat*
- Plastic gloves (optional)

*Used in this project: Makin's Clay Professional Ultimate Clay Extruder, Walnut Hollow glass cutting mat.

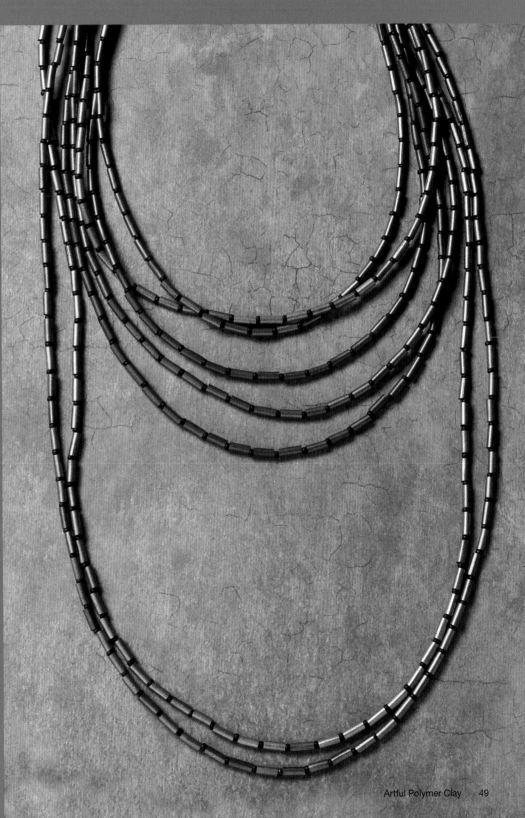

This builds on the Tube Bead Necklace project to create many strands of various metallic colors. I designed this project so the color strands can be changed easily; you will need only one clasp.

INSTRUCTIONS

1. Using black clay, follow the instructions for the Tube Bead Necklace (steps 1–5, p. 48) until you have extruded all of the clay into tubes. Cut the tubes into lengths that will fit the tile.

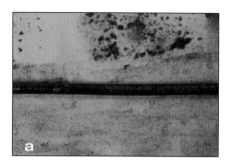

2. Dot the back of the scrap paper with one of the colors of powdered pigment. Gently roll a tube of clay on the powdered pigment. **(a)**

3. Continue rolling the tube in the powder until the tube is covered. Roll gently; do not press down on the clay, as this may close the hole in the center.

4. Repeat with additional tubes until you have enough to complete your necklace.

5. Bake for one hour and cool.

6. Rub the tubes with a paper towel to remove any excess powder.

7. Repeat with any other colors as desired.

8. Cut the tubes into ¼-in. (6 mm) beads with a craft knife. **(b)**

9. String the beads on a length of beading wire, adding seed beads as desired. If you want to make multiple strands, make them all slightly different lengths. Add a crimp bead and a split ring to each end, go back through the crimp bead, and crimp to finish (see p. 10). Hang individual strands on an S-hook.

tip
If you get powder on your fingers, it will wash off easily. If you like, wear plastic gloves to protect your hands.

tip
To cut a lot of beads comfortably, add a clay handle to your needle tool.

tip

For earrings, string seed beads and tube beads on a length of wire. String a crimp bead on each wire end, and string a split ring through both ends. Go back through the crimp beads and crimp. Add an earring wire to the split ring to finish. Repeat to make a second earring.

Magic Square Beads

MATERIALS
- Polymer clay:
  Gold
  Blue
  Pearl
- Beading wire
- 2 crimp beads
- Clasp
- Coordinating beads
- 2 3-in. (7.6 cm) head pins
- Pair ear wires

TOOLS
- Clay machine or acrylic roller
- Slicing blade or craft knife
- Needle tool
- Ceramic tile covered with polyester batting
- Roundnose pliers
- Chainnose pliers
- Wire cutters
- Clay extruder*
- Clay-marking ruler*
- Water bottle or small circle cutter (optional)
- Paper towel

*Used in this project: Makin's Clay Professional Ultimate Clay Extruder, Marxit by Kato.

This is a fun technique: Place layers of clay in the extruder to form a great multicolored pattern. Choose any number of shades, and try using multiple thicknesses of clay sheets to vary the effect. I show two different ways to fill the extruder—but remember, just have fun!

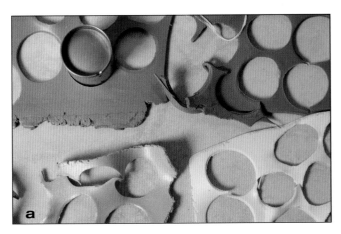

a

b

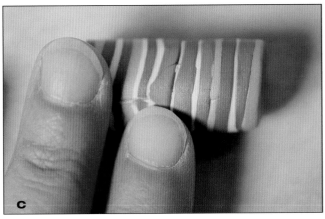

c

d

INSTRUCTIONS

Condition and completely mix some of the blue clay with some of the gold clay to create green (see p. 6). Add either more gold or blue clay to half the green mix to create a lighter or darker green. Condition the remaining gold clay and the pearl clay separately. Create a sheet of each color, slightly varying the thicknesses.

Method 1

1. Use the extruder barrel to cut varying colors of clay by pressing the barrel into the clay and keeping each color in the barrel as you work. After you have three or four circles, mist the other end of the barrel with water. The moisture will help the discs slide up the barrel.

2. Continue cutting and stacking colors as far as possible. With this method, it can be difficult to fill the entire barrel.

Method 2

1. Use the small circle cutter to cut various colors of clay. When the cutter is almost full, push the clay out of the cutter and set aside. **(a)**

2. Repeat step 1. (Sometimes the discs won't stay in the cutter. That's fine—just set them aside and stack later.) **(b)**

3. Place the discs together. Roll them to reduce the thickness until they will fit inside the extruder. **(c)**

4. Place the rolled discs in the extruder barrel. **(d)**

e

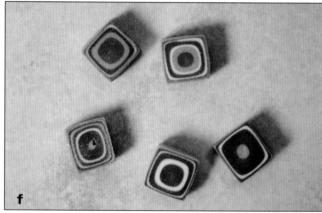

f

Finishing

1. When the extruder barrel is filled, place the square disc and end cap on the barrel. Screw the extruder portion onto the other end of the barrel. **(e)**

2. Extrude the clay. Cut this clay into strip that are the same length as the clay-marking ruler. Press the strips on the 5 mm side of the clay-marking ruler with just enough pressure to mark the strip.

3. Use a slicing blade to cut the beads at the marks. Clean the blade with a wet paper towel if it starts to drag or pull the colors together. Use a needle tool to make a hole through the top center of each bead. **(f)**

4. Bake for one hour. Cool.

5. String the clay beads, alternating with coordinating beads, until you reach the desired length. String a crimp bead and half of a clasp on each end. Go back through the crimp beads, crimp, and trim any excess wire (see p. 10).

6. To make an earring, string clay beads and coordinating beads on a head pin in the desired pattern. Make a plain loop and attach it to an ear wire (see p. 10). Repeat for the second earring.

tip

The clay takes the path of least resistance as it is extruded, so the clay over the hole gets pushed out before the clay on the sides, where the metal disc inhibits the push. This creates the color patterns.

Magic Square Beads Set

MATERIALS
- Polymer clay:
  Gold
  Blue
  Pearl
  Copper
- Beading wire
- Assorted seed beads
- Clasp
- 2 crimp beads
- 2 2-in. (5 cm) head pins
- Pair earring wires

TOOLS
- Clay machine or acrylic roller
- Silicone roller
- Slicing blade or craft knife
- Needle tool
- Clay shaper
- Ceramic tile covered with polyester batting
- Roundnose pliers
- Chainnose pliers
- Crimping pliers
- Wire cutters
- Flex-blade (optional)
- Nylon scouring pad or rough sandpaper

After you have made the Magic Square Beads, try this option to make a detailed pendant and earrings set using combined extruded slices.

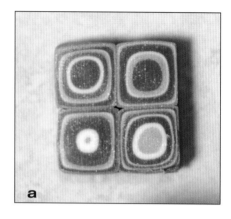

a

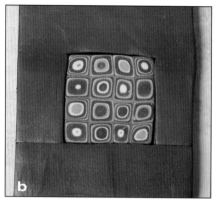

b

INSTRUCTIONS

1. This pendant builds on the extruding technique on p. 54. Follow the instructions to extrude the clay. Cut one 5-in. (13 cm) length, but do not mark.

2. Cut the 5-in. (13 cm) strip in half, lay the two halves next to each other, and gently press together. Cut this segment in half, and lay one half on top of the other. Gently press together.

3. Cut two slices from this stack for earrings and four slices for a pendant. **(a)** Lay the four slices together to form a pendant four squares by four squares.

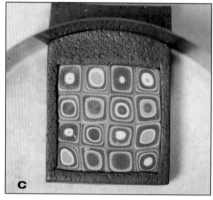

c

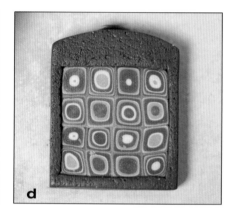

d

4. Condition the copper-colored clay and run it through the clay machine at the thickest setting.

5. Place the pendant piece cut in step 3 on the copper sheet. Cut four strips at least ½-in. (1.3 cm) wide, and lay one strip next to the four-slice square. Trim the excess clay at the edge of the square. Place two pieces butted up to the first piece. Trim and place the last piece so that the square in enclosed in clay. Smooth the seams. **(b)**

6. Trim three edges close to the square. Use a flex-blade or craft knife to cut a curved top as shown. **(c)**

7. Texture the copper clay with the scouring pad or sandpaper. Pierce a hole from side to side at the top using a needle tool. **(d)**

8. Repeat steps 4–7 with one slice for an earring bead, except make all sides equal and pierce the hole through the center of the piece from top to bottom. Repeat to make a second earring bead.

9. Bake all pieces for one hour. Cool.

10. Center the pendant on a length of beading wire. Follow step 5 on page 54 to finish the necklace.

11. To finish an earring, string a seed bead, an earring bead, a seed bead, a small Magic Square Bead, and a seed bead on a head pin. Make a simple loop and attach to an earring wire (see p. 10). Repeat to make a second earring.

tip

When cutting clay, the top edges will round slightly due to the pressure from the knife, and the bottom will have a straight cut. Turn cut pieces over and use the bottom for a better fit.

Plum Necklace and Earrings

MATERIALS

- Polymer clay:
  Silver
  Red or red concentrate
- Beading wire
- Seed beads in
  3 coordinating colors
- 2 crimp beads
- Toggle clasp
- 2 head pins
- 2 ear wires

TOOLS

- Clay machine or acrylic
  roller
- Silicone roller
- Slicing blade or craft
  knife
- Needle tool
- Clay shaper
- Ball stylus
- Ceramic tile covered with
  polyester batting
- Roundnose pliers
- Chainnose pliers
- Wire cutters
- Circle cutter set*
- Wavy cutter

Used in this project: Makin's Clay Cutter set.

tip

Concentrated color allows the mica properties to be more intense.

This is the first of three techniques you can use to create a chatoyant effect. The lovely necklace will definitely get you noticed!

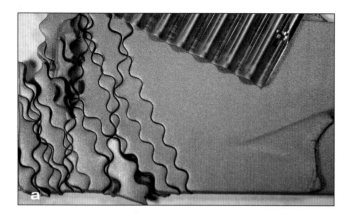

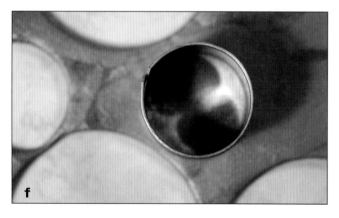

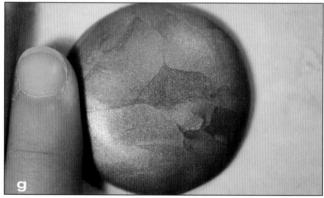

INSTRUCTIONS

1. Condition the silver clay (see p. 6), adding the red concentrate until you like the color. Run it through the clay machine on the thickest setting to create a sheet of clay. Cut this sheet in half and stack the two halves.

2. Cut the sheet into pieces with the wavy cutter. **(a)**

3. Separate the pieces. **(b)** Form the pieces into a loose pile of clay. **(c)**

4. Flatten the clay using a rubber brayer or silicone roller. **(d)**

5. Run the sheet created through the clay machine at the thickest setting. **(e)**

6. Cut three large circles for the pendant and two smaller circles for each earring. **(f)** Stack the circles.

7. Round the edges of each circle stack with your fingers. **(g)**

8. Pierce the pendant bead near the top of the bead and through the center of the earring beads using a needle tool.

9. Bake all of the pieces upside down for one hour. Cool.

10. Thread three strands of beading wire through the pendant. String seed beads on each strand. Thread all three strands through three final seed beads on each end. On each end, string a crimp bead and half of the clasp. Go back through the crimp bead and a few beads. Crimp the crimp beads and trim any excess wire (see p. 10).

Chatoyant Switch Plate

MATERIALS
- Polymer clay:
  Gold
  Pearl
- Scrap clay in any color
- Metal switch plate

TOOLS
- Clay machine or acrylic roller
- Silicone roller
- Slicing blade or craft knife
- Needle tool
- Clay shaper
- Ceramic tile covered with polyester batting
- Grater used for clay only
- High-gloss varnish* (optional)

*Used in this project: Plaid's FolkArt Polyurethane Gloss Artists' Varnish.

Try this second technique to get a chatoyant effect for a sparkly home decoration. The project doesn't require a metal plate for each cover, since it is just used as a form. If you want to keep the metal plate, skip to step 4.

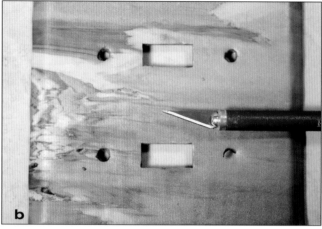

INSTRUCTIONS

1. Condition the scrap clay (see p. 6) and run it through the clay machine on the thickest setting, creating a sheet large enough to cover the metal switch plate. **(a)**

2. Cover the metal switch plate and trim the excess clay at the edges and switch holes with a craft knife. Use the clay shaper or a narrow paintbrush handle to pierce the clay over the screw holes. **(b)**

3. Keep the clay on the switch plate and bake for 30 minutes. Cool.

4. Condition and completely mix equal parts gold and pearl clay. Form this mixture into a ball. It does not have to be a smooth ball; just squish the clay together. **(c)**

5. Shred the clay using the grater. **(d)**

tip

Remember, items used with clay should not be used for food.

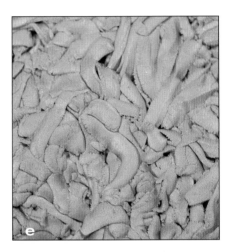

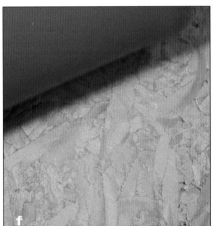

6. Combine the shredded clay into a loose ball. **(e)**

7. Flatten the clay with your hands, then with a soft roller (rubber or silicone). (A hard acrylic roller will realign the mica particles in a different direction. Use it if necessary, but do so gently.) **(f)**

8. Using a thickness setting that is slightly thinner than the clay sheet, run the sheet through the clay machine once, reduce the thickness by one, turn the sheet, and run it through a second time.

9. Cover the scrap clay with this sheet and trim.

10. Bake upside down on the ceramic tile covered with polyester batting. If any air bubbles occur, immediately after removing the piece from the oven, place it on a flat, smooth surface and press down. Cover with a weight, such as a book, and allow the piece to cool.

11. Remove the clay from the metal switch plate. The chatoyant effect is more noticeable if the clay is shiny, so cover with several coats of a high-gloss varnish, or sand and buff, if desired.

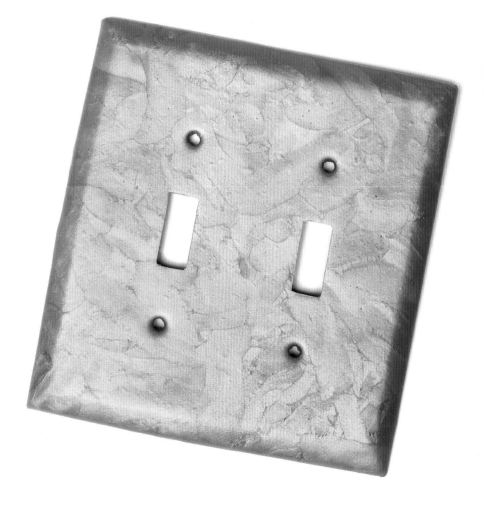

Covered
Mint Tin

MATERIALS
- Polymer clay:
  Metallic gold
  Blue concentrate
- Metal mint tin

TOOLS
- Clay machine or acrylic roller
- Silicone roller
- Slicing blade or craft knife
- Needle tool
- Ceramic tile covered with polyester batting
- Art mold*
- Spray bottle with water
- Hot pad

*Used in this project: Krafty Lady AMKT4 Rococo Texture art mold.

Here's a third technique for creating the chatoyant effect with metallic clay. It takes a little practice to achieve great results, but the effort is well worth it.

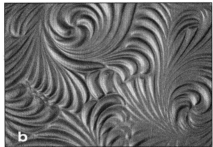

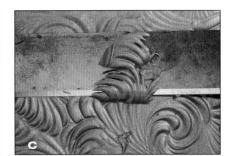

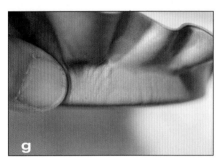

INSTRUCTIONS

1. Condition and mix the gold clay with a small amount of blue concentrate (see p. 6). Using the concentrated color will keep the metallic mica from being diluted. (If concentrated color is not available, you can use regular blue clay.) Add color until you have the desired green. Run the clay through the clay machine on a medium setting.

2. Place the texture mold face up with the clay on top of the sheet. To keep your fingers from sticking and pulling the clay up off the mold, mist the clay with water. Press the clay firmly to the texture mold. Continue pressing the clay to the mold until the entire mold is full. **(a)**

3. Wipe any remaining water off the clay sheet. Remove the sheet of clay from the texture mold and place it face up on the tile. Gently press the clay to the tile. **(b)**

4. Hold the slicing blade in both hands and slightly curve the blade. Slice off the raised clay. Continue slicing off the raised portion until it is completely removed. You can remove some of the non-raised portion, but don't carve too deep. This takes some practice. If by chance you cut too deep, just recondition the clay and try again. **(c)**

5. Run the sheet through the clay machine at a medium setting. Turn the sheet 90 degrees and run it through at one setting thinner. If the top is not smooth, repeat. **(d)**

6. Place the clay sheet on the top of the tin. Start from the middle and press the clay to the edge of the tin, smoothing out any air bubbles. Press the clay over the edge of the tin. **(e)**

7. Gently work any excess clay smooth, starting at the top and working to the edge. **(f)**

8. Make sure the edges are smooth. **(g)** Trim the excess with a slicing blade or craft knife.

9. Bake the tin top. Check for any air bubbles while it is still warm, and press them out with a hot pad. Cool.

10. Recondition the excess clay and run it through the clay machine, reducing the thickness until you reach the same setting used for the top. Place the top on the can, and then cover the bottom with clay. Trim the clay where the top meets the bottom. Remove the top and press the clay slightly up the edge. This will give you a completely covered can with no metal showing. Check that the top will still fit and the can is completely covered.

11. Bake the bottom and cool. Add mints for a delicious treat!

Mosaic Flower Coasters

MATERIALS

- Polymer clay:
  White
- Powdered pigments:*
  Lavender
  Yellow
- Instant tacky glue*
- Cork circle

*Used in this project: Pearl-Ex
Powdered Pigments by Jaquard in
Misty Lavender and Brilliant Yellow and
Crafter's Pick Ultimate Tacky Glue.

TOOLS

- Clay machine or acrylic
  roller
- Slicing blade or craft
  knife
- Needle tool
- Clay shaper
- Ceramic tile
- 4-in. (10 cm) circle cutter
- Flower stencil*
- Pasta or clay machine
  with small noodle
  attachment
- Ruler and craft knife
  (optional)

*Used in this project: Delta Traditional
Daisies Stencil.

Capture the essence of a detailed mosaic! Polymer clay is an excellent material for creating mosaics because it's easy to cut and you don't need any special tools or protective eyewear.

INSTRUCTIONS

1. Condition the white polymer clay (see p. 6), and run it through your clay machine at the thickest setting. Place the sheet on a ceramic tile. Place the circle cutter on the clay sheet and trim around it with a craft knife to make the coaster base. Save the excess clay for the color mix.

2. Center a flower stencil on the base and use a needle tool to trace around the pattern. Remove the stencil. **(a)**

3. Condition the excess clay and run it through the clay machine at a medium setting. Cut a 3-in. (7.6 cm) square of clay and a 2-in. (5 cm) square of clay. Add lavender powdered pigment to the larger square and yellow powder pigment to the smaller square.

4. Roll and twist the lavender clay into a long snake to mix in all of the pigment. Form the snake into a ball and roll the clay into a snake again, twisting the snake as you roll. Repeat two or three times.

5. Flatten the clay with your fingers and run it through the clay machine on the thickest setting. Reduce the thickness by one setting and run the sheet through again. Repeat until you reach the #6 setting, turning the sheet, if desired, to create a nice pattern. Run this sheet through the small noodle attachment, or cut thin strips using a ruler and craft knife. Repeat steps 4 and 5 with the yellow clay to make noodles.

6. Place several lavender noodles on the ceramic tile and cut them into small pieces with your craft knife. Use the knife to pick up and place pieces along the edges of the petal, leaving a small

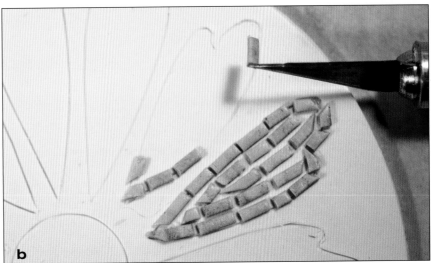

space between pieces. Trim the pieces where necessary to make them fit. **(b)**

7. Fill in the center of the flower with yellow in a similar way. Continue to fill in the rest of the petals and center of the flower, using the appropriate colors, until you have filled in the entire pattern.

8. Firmly but gently, press the mosaic pieces on the base with your hands to make sure they all adhere.

9. Bake for 30–60 minutes. Cool completely on the ceramic tile. To remove, gently slide the slicing blade under the pieces.

10. Center the coaster on the cork circle. Glue the coaster to the cork, pressing gently to remove any air bubbles.

Mosaic Votive Holder

MATERIALS
- Polymer clay:
  Translucent
  Pearl
  Gold
- Square glass votive

TOOLS
- Clay machine or acrylic roller
- Slicing blade or craft knife
- Needle tool
- Clay shaper
- Ceramic tile covered with polyester batting
- Clay extruder*

*Used in this project: Makin's Clay Ultimate Extruder with the #8 disc.

Create an ivory mosaic votive with translucent beauty. With this technique, you can make shell-like decorative votives with ease.

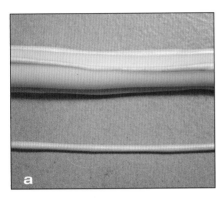

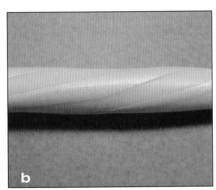

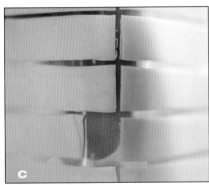

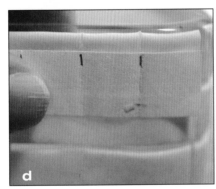

INSTRUCTIONS

1. Condition translucent polymer clay and a small amount of pearl clay separately (see p. 6). Run a sheet of each through the clay machine at the thickest setting.

2. Form a thick snake with the translucent clay and three or four thin noodles with the pearl clay. Place the noodles, evenly spaced, around the translucent pearl snake. **(a)**

3. Roll the snake until smooth, twisting it as you roll. Fold in half and repeat twice. **(b)**

4. Fold into quarters, flatten, and run the clay through the clay machine at a medium setting. Place the clay on the tile and cut into ½-in. (1.3 cm) strips.

5. Starting at the top of the glass, lay the strips horizontally and evenly spaced, trimming where the strips meet. Keep laying strips down the glass, leaving a small gap between the strips. (If a strip is not long enough to go all the way around the votive, wait until after step 7 to add a piece of clay.) **(c)**

6. Using a craft knife, mark every ½ in. (1.3 cm) on the top clay strip. **(d)**

7. Place the slicing blade across the strips, from the top to the bottom and cut twice, slightly apart along the previous marks. Repeat on the other three sides. If you have any small sections where the strip was short, add the piece now and match the previous cuts. **(e)**

8. Using a needle tool, remove the small strips to leave tiles of clay. **(f)**

9. Condition and mix equal parts pearl and gold clay. Form this into a log and place it into the extruder with the #8 disc. Extrude long clay noodles.

10. Gently press the extruded noodles in the spaces from the top to the bottom of the glass. **(g)**

11. Use a clay shaper to press the noodles down between the tiles. **(h)**

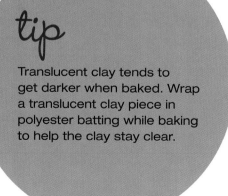

12. Place more noodles around the glass vertically, trimming clay where the noodles meet. Smooth the seams.

13. Bake for 30 minutes. Cool completely on the ceramic tile.

tip

Translucent clay tends to get darker when baked. Wrap a translucent clay piece in polyester batting while baking to help the clay stay clear.

More Inspirational Ideas

Use a triangle disc with the extruder adaptor to make hollow snakes. Twist the extruded snakes to make this jewelry set. To add memory wire to an extruded piece, warm the baked clay, form it into a circle, and then string on memory wire.

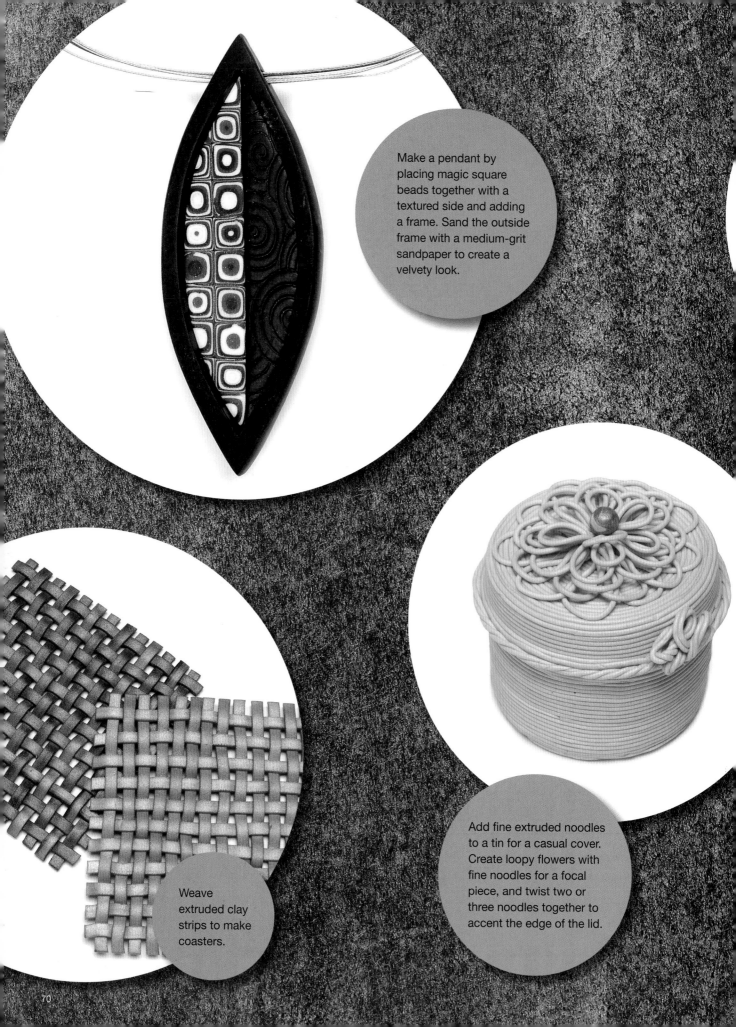

Make a pendant by placing magic square beads together with a textured side and adding a frame. Sand the outside frame with a medium-grit sandpaper to create a velvety look.

Add fine extruded noodles to a tin for a casual cover. Create loopy flowers with fine noodles for a focal piece, and twist two or three noodles together to accent the edge of the lid.

Weave extruded clay strips to make coasters.

Cover a tin using two or more colors of chatoyant clay separated by black strips.

Create this vase in the same way you created the votive. Run a thin sheet through a clay machine, and place individual pieces on the glass. Decorate the top with curved accents.

Combine colored strips of chatoyant clay and accent with black strips. Bake and glue to a checkbook cover.

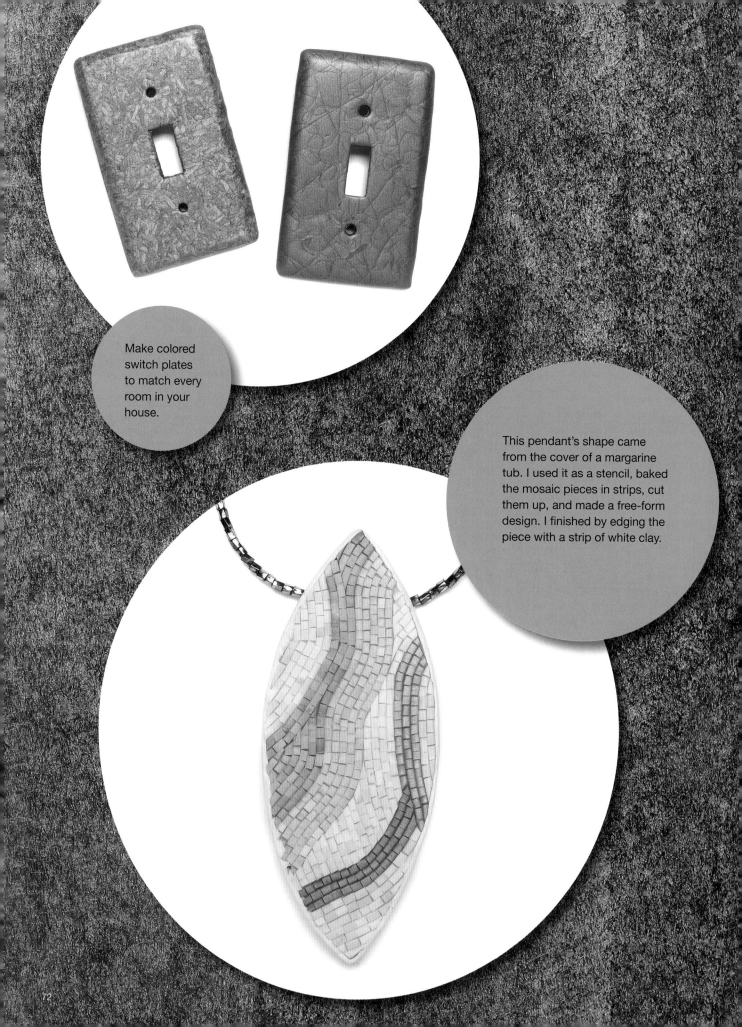

Make colored switch plates to match every room in your house.

This pendant's shape came from the cover of a margarine tub. I used it as a stencil, baked the mosaic pieces in strips, cut them up, and made a free-form design. I finished by edging the piece with a strip of white clay.

Mokume gane is an ancient Japanese technique for layering and forging metals, then carving them to expose different layers. Polymer clay artists have adapted this technique to great effect.

The mokume gane projects in this book show three different ways to produce this fun effect. There is no "correct" technique for mokume gane. Adjust or try your own thing. Just remember to avoid making the layers too thin, or you may lose the beautiful effect of this technique.

Mokume Gane and Combined Techniques

Heart Pendant, Earrings, and Bracelet

MATERIALS
- Polymer clay:
  Magenta
  Pearl
  Silver
- Silver leaf
- Silver-plated beading wire
- Toggle clasp
- 2 crimp beads
- 2 2-in. (5 cm) head pins
- 2 ear wires
- Metal bracelet blank

TOOLS
- Clay machine or acrylic roller
- Silicone roller
- Slicing blade or craft knife
- Needle tool
- Clay shaper
- Ceramic tile covered with polyester batting
- Roundnose pliers
- Chainnose pliers
- Wire cutters
- Crimping pliers
- 2 or 3 paintbrushes with various handle sizes
- Metal ruler or plastic card

tip

You can find bracelet blanks in different shapes and widths at your local dollar store.

This jewelry set incorporates one technique for making mokume gane. Make a collection with ease!

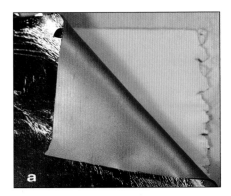

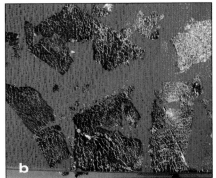

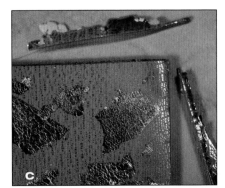

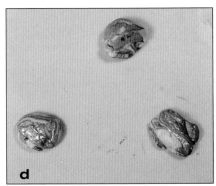

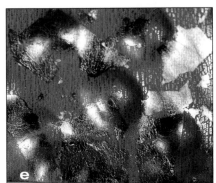

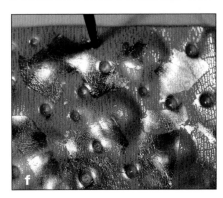

INSTRUCTIONS

Pendant and earrings

1. Condition and completely mix ¼ part white, ¼ part silver, and ½ part pearl clay (see p. 6). Run through the clay machine at the #3 setting to make a magenta mix.

2. Condition the excess pearl clay separately. Run through the clay machine at the #3 setting.

3. Place the pearl clay on a ceramic tile. Cut a 5½–6-in. (14–15 cm)

square. Cover the pearl clay with the magenta mix. Press the silver leaf on the magenta mix. **(a)**

4. Run the stack through the clay machine at the #3 setting. Cut the stack in half, add silver leaf to one half, and cover with the other half.

5. Repeat step 4 twice. Use the #5 setting for the second pass through the clay machine. Cut the clay in half and add leaf. Cut in the opposite direction and stack again. **(b)**

6. Trim the uneven edges. **(c)**

7. Cut the trimmed edges into pieces and roll them into rough balls. Turn the stack over and randomly place the balls on the stack. **(d)**

8. Turn the stack back over and press the clay down around the balls. **(e)**

9. Press the end of a paintbrush randomly on the stack. Use brushes with different sized handles for variety. **(f)**

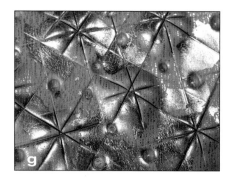

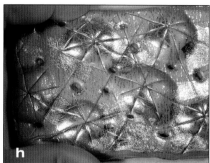

10. Using a metal ruler or plastic card, cut across the raised areas as shown to make an interesting pattern in the clay. **(g)**

11. Pick up the stack and compress it by pushing on the sides. Doing this will help avoid round holes in slices. Press the stack to the tile. **(h)**

12. Using the slicing blade, cut fine, thin slices from the stack. Curving the blade slightly by pulling up on the ends is helpful. **(i)**

13. Form a ball from the excess magenta mix. Place the slices around this ball. **(j)**

14. Continue adding slices until the ball is covered. Roll smooth. **(k)**

15. Form the ball into the desired pendant shape. Repeat with smaller balls for earrings. **(l)**

16. Drill a hole through the pendant from side to side and through the earring beads from top to bottom. Bake for one hour.

17. String the pendant on a length of beading wire. String a crimp bead and half of a clasp on each end, go back through the crimp, and crimp (see p. 10). Trim any excess wire.

18. String an earring bead on a head pin, make a plain loop, and attach to an ear wire. Repeat for the second earring.

tip

Many other instructions for this technique call for a solid-color ball instead of using the trimmed edges. I used the edges so when you slice through the stack, eventually there will not be a solid-colored circle in the slice. Either way is fine.

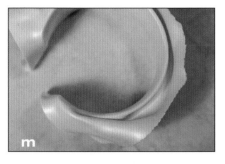

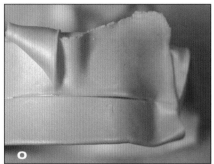

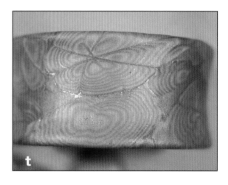

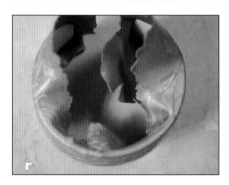

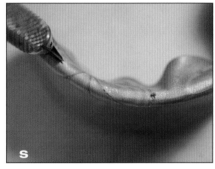

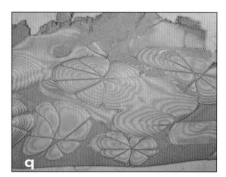

Bracelet

1. Run the excess pearl clay through the clay machine at the #6 setting. Cut one long edge straight. Cover the bracelet blank, starting with the cut edge centered on the front of the blank. Wrap the clay around the inside of the blank and back to the front. **(m)**

2. Smooth the clay, removing any trapped air. **(n)**

3. Press the clay against the cut edge. Trim the excess and smooth the seam. **(o)** Bake for one hour and cool.

4. Run magenta clay through the clay machine at the #6 setting. Make a sheet slightly larger than the bracelet blank. Add pieces cut from the mokume gane stack to cover the pearl clay. Use the brayer to smooth the pieces. **(p, q)**

5. Continue adding pieces until the sheet is covered. Run through the clay machine at the #5 setting, width-wise if possible, then through at the #6 setting. Turn the sheet 90 degrees and run through at the #7 setting.

6. Cover the front edge of the pearl clay cuff, pressing to remove the air and over the edge toward the back. **(r)**

7. Trim the excess clay. The bracelet will have a pearl underside. **(s)**

8. Smooth if necessary. Bake and cool. **(t)**

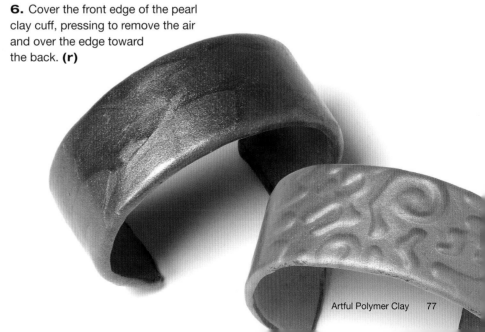

Covered Pen and Notebook

MATERIALS

- Polymer clay:
  Turquoise
  2 blocks gold
  Black (optional)
- Gold leaf
- Pen blank
- Notebook with wire binding

Used in this project: Boston ClayWorks Amazing Twist Pen Kit.

TOOLS

- Clay machine or acrylic roller
- Silicone roller
- Slicing blade or craft knife
- Needle tool
- Ball stylus
- Ceramic tile covered with polyester batting
- Various items to impress the clay*
- Square paper punch

Used in this project: Walnut Hollow Creative Metal Beginner Kit.

This project uses a second technique to achieve the mokume gane look. All of the techniques use layers of clay, but the number of layers, the stacking, and the way they are impressed or modified are slightly different.

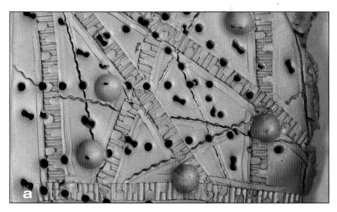

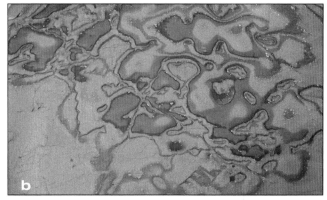

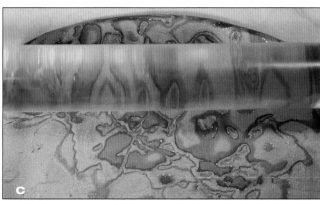

INSTRUCTIONS

Pen

1. Condition and completely mix ¼ of the turquoise block and ¼ of the gold block for the desired green (see p. 6).

2. Condition the remaining gold clay separately, then condition ⅛ of the remaining turquoise clay.

3. Run the green through the clay machine at the #4 setting. Place a 6-in. (15 cm) square on the tile. Layer a 3 x 6 in. (7.6 x 15 cm) piece of turquoise clay that has been run through the clay machine at the thinnest setting. Add a piece of gold leaf, a sheet of gold clay run at the #4 setting, gold leaf, a sheet of green run at the #5 setting, gold leaf, and then gold clay run at the #5 setting.

4. Run the stack through the clay machine at the thickest setting. Cut the stack in half, add gold leaf to half, and cover with the other half. Run through the clay machine at the thickest setting. Repeat this step once, but run the stack through at the #3 setting.

5. Cut in half and stack. Cut in half in the other direction and stack. Impress this stack using various items. **(a)**

6. Pick up the stack and compress by pushing on the sides.

7. Slice thin pieces of the stack. If the layers are too thick, use the acrylic roller to flatten the stack. After thinning, cut and stack again. **(b, c)**

tip

The pen blank used here is from Boston ClayWorks. It is by far the easiest to use, as the pieces screw together. Many other companies make pen blanks, but you may need a pen press or 6-in. (15 cm) C-clamp to put them together. Check the instructions that come with the pen blank for more information.

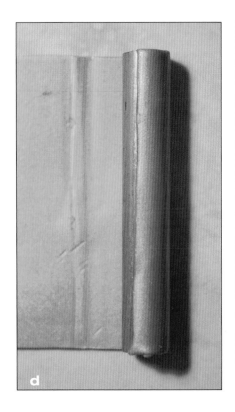

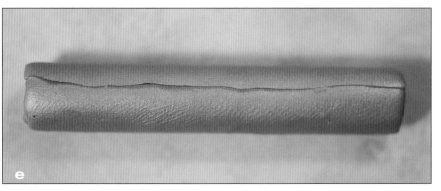

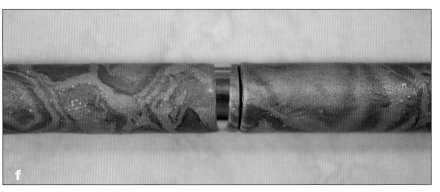

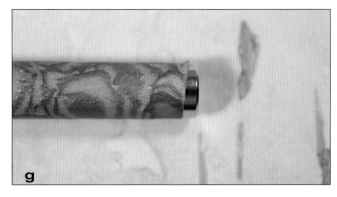

8. Run some of the excess gold clay through the clay machine at the #6 setting. Cut a strip the length of the pen blank. Cover the blank with clay. Roll the covered blank against the excess clay and roll back. Trim along the line created where the clay edges meet. **(d)**

9. Smooth the seam. **(e)**

10. Screw the pen parts together, leaving the ink cartridge out. Add thin slices from the mokume gane stack. Roll the pen between your hands. Cut the excess clay where it overlaps the pen pieces. **(f)**

11. Roll the pen on a smooth ceramic tile, using light pressure. The excess clay will stick to the tile. Use the slicing blade to remove the clay from the tile. Repeat until the pen is smooth and no excess clay is on the tile. Feel the pen to be sure there are no indents. If there are, add a slice from the stack and smooth again. **(g)**

12. Bake the pen for one hour and cool. Insert the ink cartridge.

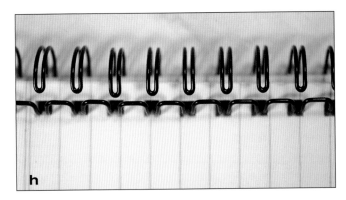

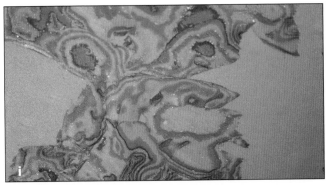

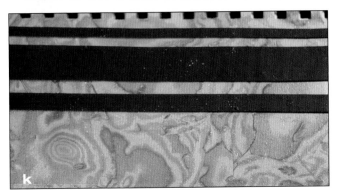

Notebook

1. Remove the covers from the notebook. The type of notebook pictured is the easiest to use. **(h)**

2. Recondition excess clay to create a gold sheet. Run through the clay machine at the medium setting to make a sheet slightly larger than the cover.

3. Layer slices from the stack on the gold sheet. Continue until the sheet is covered with clay. **(i)**

4. Roll the brayer on the clay to smooth the pieces. Reset the clay machine to the medium setting and run the sheet created through the clay machine, with the wider side against the rollers. Reduce the setting by one, turn the sheet 90 degrees, and run the sheet through again.

5. Lay the cover removed from the notebook on the sheet. Trim around the cover.

6. Using a ball stylus, mark the center of the holes on the cover. **(j)**

7. Repeat steps 2–6 for the back cover. If desired, add strips of thin black clay to the front cover. **(k)**

8. Bake both covers for one hour. If the covers are not flat, place them on a second tile or countertop while they are still warm, press to flatten, and cover with a weight. Cool.

9. Punch holes using the square punch, centering the marks made in step 6 within the square. **(l)**

10. Place the covers on the notebook.

Colorful Coasters

MATERIALS
- Polymer clay:
  Ultra blue
  Copper
  White
  Black
- Copper leaf
- Cork, 4-in. (10 cm) circle
- Tacky glue*

*Used in this project: Crafter's Pick Ultimate Tacky Glue.

TOOLS
- Clay machine
- Acrylic roller
- Silicone roller
- Slicing blade
- Craft knife
- Needle tool
- Clay shaper
- Ball stylus
- Ceramic tile covered with polyester batting
- Beginner metal tool kit*
- Old credit card or metal ruler
- 4-in. (10 cm) round cutter

*Used in this project: Walnut Hollow Creative Metal Beginner Tool Kit.

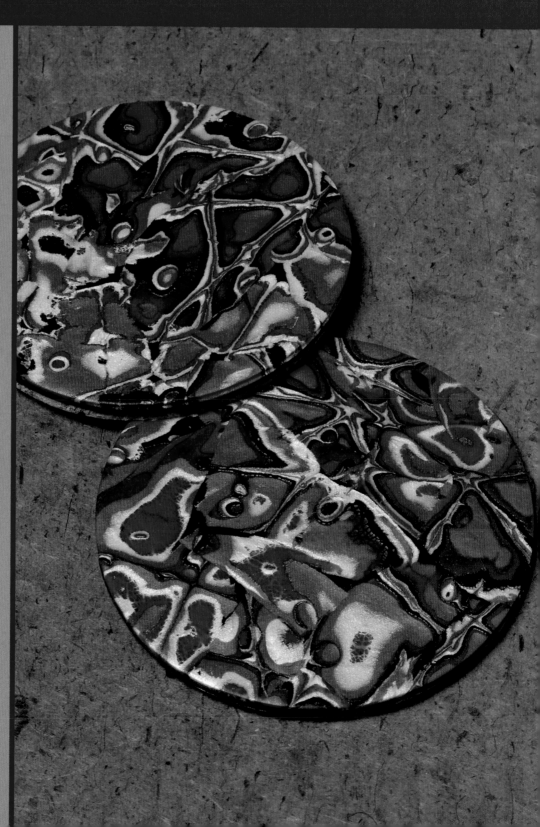

This mokume gane technique is similar to the one used for the Covered Pen and Notebook. This project uses different colors and slightly thicker sheets for a dramatic look.

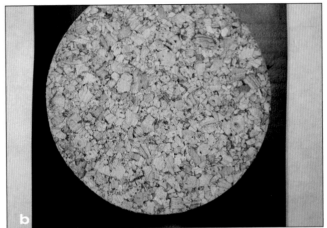

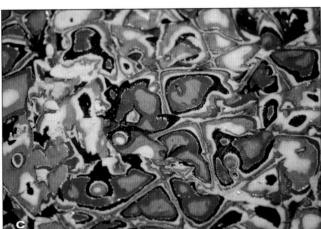

INSTRUCTIONS

1. Condition all the colors of clay separately (see p. 6). Run them through the clay machine at a medium setting. Run the black sheet through again at a thinner setting.

2. Cut the sheets into small pieces and stack the four colors, alternating with the copper leaf in any order desired.

3. Run the stack through the clay machine at the thickest setting. Cut the stack in half, and add copper leaf to half. Cover with the other half. Run this stack through the clay machine again at the thickest setting.

4. Cut in half and stack. Cut in half in the other direction. Impress this stack using the credit card and metal tools. **(a)**

5. Compress the stack by pushing on the sides.

6. Recondition the excess black clay and run it through on the thickest setting. Cut a piece of clay slightly larger than the cork. **(b)**

7. Layer slices from the stack on the black sheet. Continue until the sheet is covered with clay as desired. **(c)**

8. Roll the brayer on the clay to smooth the pieces. Run the sheet created through the clay machine at the thickest setting, with the wider side against the rollers. Reduce the setting by one, turn the sheet 90 degrees, and run the sheet through again.

9. Lay the sheet on a conditioned sheet of black clay.

10. Cut out a coaster using the cookie cutter. **(d)**

11. Smooth the coaster edges, if necessary. Bake for one hour and cool. Glue a cork circle to the back of the coaster.

Leafy Tablet Cover

Kato Liquid Polyclay is strong and flexible enough for this technique. It will also level itself. Test your liquid clay before beginning this project to ensure that it is strong and flexible.

MATERIALS

- Polymer clay:
  2 blocks black
  Gold
  Turquoise
- Liquid clay*
- Powdered pigment*
- 3½ x 5 in. (8.9 x 13 cm) tablet of paper

*Used in this project: Kato Liquid, Pearl-Ex by Jacquard: Macropearl.

TOOLS

- Clay machine or acrylic roller
- Silicone roller
- Slicing blade or craft knife
- Needle tool
- Clay shaper
- Ceramic tile covered with polyester batting
- Toothpick
- Leaf art mold*
- Stamping wheel*
- Cardboard
- Nonstick aluminum foil
- Small disposable plastic cup or bowl
- Ruler
- Decorative scissors (optional)

*Used in this project: Krafty Lady Art Mold: AM337 Three Leaves; Clearsnap Jumbo Rollagraph Stamp Wheel: Leafy Border.

This technique takes full advantage of the strength and flexibility of liquid clay to form a hinge. Tony Aquino of VanAken International came up with the idea—thanks, Tony!

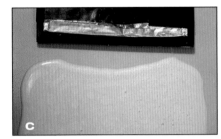

INSTRUCTIONS

Make tablet pocket

1. Cut a piece of cardboard ¼ in. (6 mm) larger than the tablet of paper. Cover the cardboard with aluminum foil.

2. Condition black clay and run it through the clay machine at the thickest setting (see p. 6). Place the foil-covered cardboard on the clay. Trim the top edge of the clay just above the foil. **(a)**

3. Trim the excess black clay on the remaining edges, gather it into a ball, and run it through the clay machine at a medium setting to make a new sheet. Cut one edge straight.

4. Unfold the foil on the top edge of the cardboard, and place the new sheet of clay on the foil ¼ in. (6 mm) down from the cut edge on the base clay.

5. Press the new clay over the edge of the base clay to seal the clay pieces together and make a pocket. Trim with the slicing blade, leaving approximately ⅛ in. (3 mm) of overlap. **(b)**

Make liquid clay hinge

1. Squirt some liquid clay into a plastic cup (about ½ in./1.3 cm deep). Mix a small amount of powdered pigment into the liquid until it is a nice pearl color (about ⅛–¼ teaspoon).

2. Pour the liquid on a smooth ceramic tile, making sure it spreads wider than the black base and more than 3½ in. (8.9 cm) long. **(c)**

3. Tap the underside of the tile to encourage air bubbles to rise. Use the needle tool or a toothpick to prick any bubbles. Clean the tip or use a new toothpick as needed.

4. Bake the liquid clay for 30 minutes. Cool. The tile side of the liquid is the usable side.

5. Using a craft knife and a ruler, trim the liquid sheet straight on two ends so it is the same width as the pocket. On the other ends, cut one end straight, or use decorative scissors to make a textured edge. Measure 3–3¼ in. (7.6–8.3 cm), and using a craft knife, cut the last end straight.

Add gold front

1. Condition the gold clay and run it through the clay machine at a medium setting. Cut a gold sheet the same size as the black base. Impress the clay with an uninked stamping wheel. **(d)**

2. Place the pocket, foil side down, on a large ceramic tile. Place the gold piece, stamped side up, 1 in. (2.5 cm) away from the base. (Make sure the open part of the pocket faces the gold.) Center the hinge on top of the two pieces. Spread a small amount of liquid clay on the back side of the hinge where it overlaps the clay sheets. Note: the side of the liquid that was on the tile during baking is now the top/front of the sheet. **(e)**

Decorate and finish cover

1. Mix some turquoise clay into some of the excess gold clay until you have a pleasing yellow-green. Form the leaves using an art mold, and arrange them on the front of the cover. **(f)**

2. Bake for one hour and cool.

3. Try to pull the foil and cardboard out. If necessary, unwrap the foil at the top, gently pull out the cardboard, and remove the foil.

4. Insert a tablet into the back.

Extruded Beads and Mokume Gane

MATERIALS

- Polymer clay: Translucent White
- Liquid clay
- Alcohol inks in green and blue*
- Silver leaf
- 6 in. (15 cm) 20-gauge silver wire
- Beading wire
- 2 crimp tubes
- Silver toggle
- 2 ear wires
- White glass beads

*Used in this project: Ranger Adirondack Alcohol Ink: Meadow, Wild Plum, and Stonewashed.

TOOLS

- Clay machine or acrylic roller
- Silicone roller
- Slicing blade or craft knife
- Needle tool
- Ceramic tile covered with polyester batting
- Roundnose pliers
- Chainnose pliers
- Wire cutters
- Clay extruder and 1 mm extruder adaptor*
- Glass cutting mat*
- Paintbrush

*Used in this project: Makin's Clay Professional Ultimate Clay Extruder, 1 mm Makin's Professional ClayCore, and Walnut Hollow glass cutting mat.

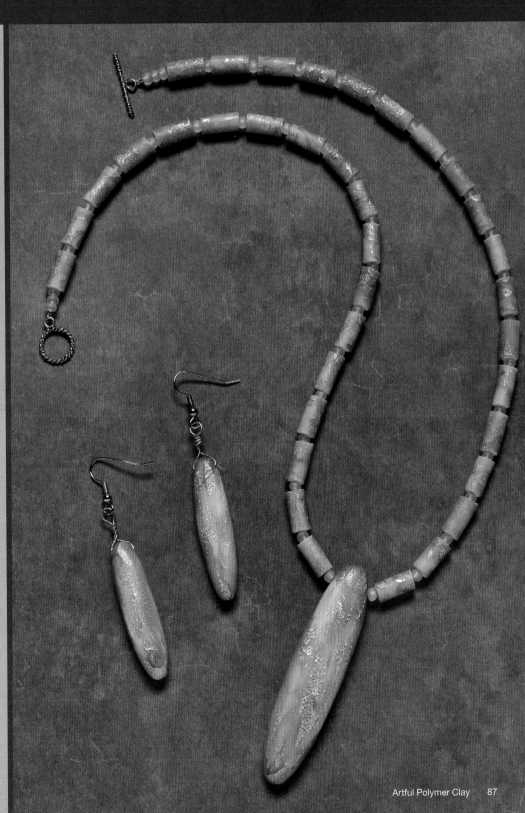

Combining two of the great techniques in this book, extruded beads and mokume gane, offers a sophisticated look.

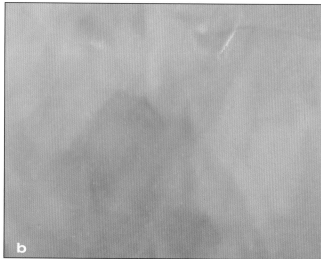

INSTRUCTIONS

Make tube beads

1. Condition the white clay (see p. 6). Roll it into a thick snake and place in the extruder with the #4 disc and the 1 mm extruder adaptor. Extrude the clay and cut it into strips to fit the tile. Taking care to keep the strips straight, place them on the polyester batting-covered tile.

2. Bake and cool.

3. Condition the translucent clay. Run the clay through the machine at the medium setting. Cut the sheet into thirds.

4. Add 5–8 drops of green alcohol ink to one third. Use a paintbrush to spread the color in loose strokes. **(a)**

5. Fold the sheet in half, and run the sheet through the clay machine at the thickest setting.

6. Repeat until you have a swirled mixture. Be sure to stop before the color is completely mixed. **(b)**

7. Repeat steps 4–6, using the purple and blue alcohol inks to color the remaining clay sections.

8. Thin each color sheet to the thinnest setting of your clay machine. If the piece gets too difficult to handle when thinning, cut it in half and thin half at a time.

9. Cut a 6-in. (15 cm) square of blue clay. Layer a sheet of silver leaf, the purple clay, a sheet of silver leaf, and the green clay. Repeat until the clay is all used, ending with the green clay. Cut in half and layer again. **(c)**

10. Impress the sheet.

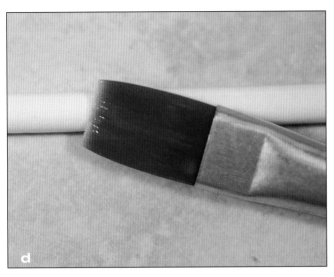

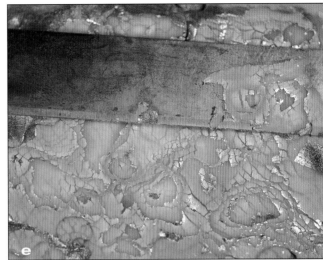

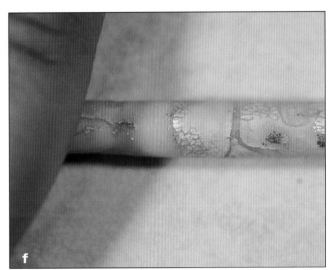

11. Brush a thin layer of liquid clay on the baked clay tubes. Let them sit about 5–10 minutes so the liquid clay is partially absorbed. **(d)**

12. Cut very thin slices off the stack of clay. **(e)**

13. Place the slices around the extruded clay tubes and roll the tubes on the tile until the piece is smooth. Feel the strips, and add extra slices or roll again until smooth if needed. **(f)**

14. Bake the tubes for one hour and cool.

15. Cut the tubes into the size beads desired with a slicing blade.

Make pendant and earring beads

1. Form a ball from the conditioned white clay. Place thin slices from your stack around this ball.

2. Continue adding slices until the ball is covered as desired. Roll smooth.

3. Form the ball into a long oval. Repeat with two smaller balls for earrings.

4. Pierce holes through the beads from side to side close to the top. Bake for one hour and cool.

Finishing

1. Center the pendant on a length of beading wire. On each end, string the mokume gane tube beads, alternating each bead with glass beads. On each end, string a crimp bead and half of the clasp. Go back through the crimp beads, and crimp (see p. 10). Trim any excess wire.

2. To make the earrings, cut two 3-in. (7.6 cm) length lengths of silver wire. Make a plain loop ½ in. (1.3 cm) away from the end of one wire (see p. 10). String an earring bead, and bend the wire up to the loop. Wrap the wire end around below the loop and attach an ear wire. Repeat to make a second earring.

tip

The clay slices will stick lightly to the slicing blade. This will help you position them.

tip

If the liquid on the extruded pieces is slippery, wait a few minutes before you work with them.

Framed Mother and Child

MATERIALS
- Polymer clay:
  Pearl
  White
  Silver
  Black
- Liquid clay or Polyglue
- Picture hanger

TOOLS
- Clay machine or acrylic roller
- Silicone roller
- Slicing blade or craft knife
- Needle tool
- Ceramic tile covered with polyester batting
- Art mold*
- Clay extruder with discs*
- Pen
- Ruler
- Piece of card stock

*Used in this project: Krafty Lady Art Mold: AM036 Madonna; Makin's Clay Professional Ultimate Clay Extruder with Ultimate Clay Extruder Discs Set B.

*Create a framed piece using three techniques:
molding clay, creating a chatoyant effect, and extruding.*

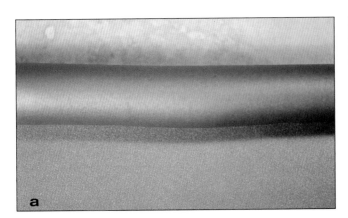

a

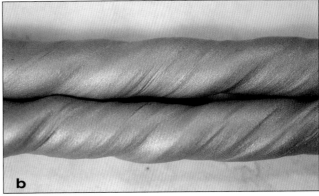

b

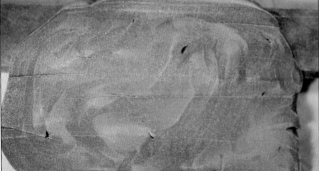

c

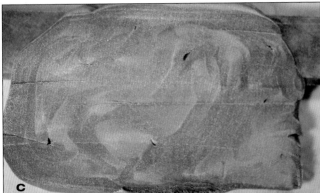

d

INSTRUCTIONS

Mold center
Condition and completely mix equal parts white and pearl clay (see p. 6). Press the clay into the art mold. Remove and set aside.

Make silver sheet
1. Condition the silver clay. Run through the clay machine at the #4 setting to make a sheet.

2. Starting at one edge, roll the sheet into a thick snake. **(a)**

3. Roll and twist the snake to give an interesting chatoyant look. **(b)**

4. Form the clay into a ball and flatten slightly. Use the slicing blade to remove the top of the ball, then cut off a sheet or two of clay. **(c)**

5. Run the sheet through the clay machine at the #5 setting. Check that the mold will fit on the sheet with at least ½ in. (1.3 cm) excess,

or the amount desired, around the mold. Place the sheet on a ceramic tile, and temporarily place the mold on the clay. Don't press to adhere the molded piece to the sheet. **(d)**

6. Cut a strip of card stock the desired width of your clay mat. Place the strip against the molded piece and trim the excess silver clay. Repeat on the three remaining sides. Remove the molded piece, leaving the sheet on the tile, and bake the silver sheet for 20 minutes. Cool.

7. Place a ruler across the sheet from corner to corner and place a small mark in the center with a pen. Repeat with the other corners to make an X in the center of the silver sheet.

Extrude frame edges
1. Condition the black clay. Roll some into a thick snake and place it in the extruder with the #38 disc. Extrude the black clay.

e

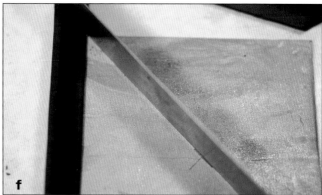
f

2. Place the extruded clay against the silver clay, with the curve of the tube next to the silver clay. Make sure the piece is straight by placing something with square sides, such as a ruler, against the extruded clay. **(e)**

3. Place a slicing blade on one of the diagonals of the X and cut the corners of the black clay. The extruded piece will need to be moved away from the sheet to complete the cut. Repeat for all four edges. **(f)**

4. Press all four black pieces against the silver sheet, pressing the corners together. Check that the corners are straight.

Add black backing

1. Rub some liquid clay on the back of the molded piece and center it on the silver sheet. Bake for 20 minutes and cool.

2. If the corners of the frame are not completely flush, press a tiny amount of black clay into the corners. Smooth with your fingers and remove any excess clay.

3. Run a sheet of black clay through the clay machine at the #3 setting. Turn the frame over and place the sheet on the clay and frame. Trim this just inside the edge. **(g)**

4. Turn over with the black side down and bake again for 20 minutes. Cool.

Finish frame

1. Sand the back to give it a matte finish.

2. Determine the center top and place the picture hanger on the back. Brush liquid clay over the edge. **(h)**

3. Run a little black clay through the clay machine at the #7 setting. Cut two rectangles and place over the edges of the hanger to secure. **(i)**

4. Bake for 20 minutes and cool.

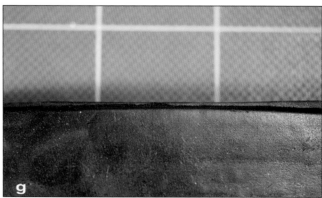
g

h

i